Tech Savvy Parenting

Brian Housman

randall house

Tech Savvy Parenting

Published by Randall House

Scripture quotations are taken from the Holy Bible, New Living Translation, copyright © 1996, 2004, 2007 by Tyndale House Foundation. Used by permission of Tyndale House Publishers, Inc., Carol Stream, Illinois 60188. All rights reserved.

ISBN-13 978-0-8926568-6-8

© 2014 by Brian Housman.

www.360Family.org

www.techsavvyparenting.com

Stockphotos used by permission of Dreamstime.com

Printed in the United States of America

Dedicated to you. Yeah, that's right, you the parent. There is no job that receives less pay, but has the highest eternal rewards.

May you count the days you have with your children and use them wisely. Don't ever forget or take lightly the privilege you've been given to be a parent.

TABLE OF CONTENTS

INTRODUCTION

There is a tension most parents feel when it comes to technology. It comes quickly hurdling at us like a tornado you can't outrun. Just when you start feeling comfortable with your iPhone, Apple releases an update with "48 new ground-breaking features." Before downloading the update, you spend days weighing whether or not you want to have to relearn to use your phone for the fifth time. You feel clueless, like a person caught in the middle of the Run of the Bulls in Pamplona as technology comes barrelling at you whether you like it or not.

In contrast, the other side of the tension comes from how quickly our children adopt new technologies into their lives. It doesn't matter if there is a new online social network, video game system, or cell phone, it all seems intuitive for your child. No instructions needed—he picks it up and starts using it as if it's always been a part of his life. Teens and tweens love to experiment with new technologies. Because teens are wired for adventure and new experiences, they quickly grow tired of doing the same thing day after day. Technology plays into that bent.

I've heard countless parents complain, "My son always has a screen in front of his face." But this generation has never known anything different. They started playing with your cell phone when they were toddlers. You probably bought them a LeapPad or similar book reader by age four. They learned how to operate the DVD player before entering kindergarten and started using computers in school by the first grade. Waging a battle against screens will only turn into a war that you will not win. **The goal isn't to abstain from screens. Instead, your desire should be moderation and responsibility with all of technology in your child's life.** This is what is at the heart of *Tech Savvy Parenting*.

Media & Personal Contentment

Effects of media usage among all 8-18 yr olds.

	Heavy Users	Moderate Users	Light Users
Make good grades (A's/B's)	51%	65%	66%
Fair/poor grades (C's & below)	47%	31%	23%
Have a lot of friends	93%	91%	91%
Get along with my parents	84%	90%	90%
Have been happy in school this year	72%	81%	82%
Am often bored	60%	81%	82%
Get into trouble a lot	33%	21%	16%
Am often sad or unhappy	32%	23%	22%

Source: Kaiser Family Foundation, M2, Media in the Lives of 8-18 Yr Olds, (c) 2010

Not only do teenagers today use technology more often than their parents, but they also multi-task at a much higher rate. In a typical week, 81% of teenagers will use part of their media time to use more than one device at a time. If they had been born with more than two hands, they could fill them each with a cell phone, game controller, computer mouse, and a PSP. The sheer magnitude of technology in your child's or teen's life will, in part, shape how they view the world, how they live in community with others, and how they plan their day-to-day activities.

As a parent, you should have great concern for how your child's life is effected by their use of technology. When we were kids, it was not uncommon to come inside only when it was time to eat dinner. To-day it seems pointless to send our children *outside* for play, because every other child in the neighborhood will be *inside* looking at a screen. Playtime has transformed into "screen time." The nature of community for 21st century teens has been radically changed. Studies confirm that excessive media is having an adverse affect on virtually every area of our children's lives. From school and grades to unhappiness and general outlook on life—media consumption plays a role.

Don't misunderstand. I'm not throwing rocks of blame at media or technology. As a matter of fact, many times technology usage is just as out of balance in our own lives. A teenager of one of my friends said, "My parents complain about how much I'm on screens, but whenever I see them their faces are glued to one as well." More than half of teenagers say that they "wish my parents would pay more attention to me and not their phone." Ouch. Even though this book is primarily about your child's use of technology, in a broader sense **it's about your whole family learning to use technology in a healthy and freeing way.**

How to Read This Book

Each chapter walks you through a different issue of technology that your child or teen is wading into. This means that you will need to wade into those deep waters as well. With the tools and resources you gather, you'll be well prepared to address these issues with your teen or child head on.

This is not a book you can simply plow through. As a matter of fact, it's probably best not to read it straight through. There is too much information—too many new things to absorb all at once. Instead, pick it up and read it when you are dealing with one of the particular areas I address. It will be much more manageable then, and it will give you time to process and practice before moving on to the next issue.

Furthermore, this is meant to be an interactive book. I want you to engage the topics with several senses. There will be times you'll be asked to write something down, such as your own plan of action. There are more than 28 photographs, 22 infographics, and 18 resources to help bring the information to life. While reading, you may be asked to do something on your phone or click on your computer. At other times you can simply absorb the statistic-filled infographics that go deeper into the subject. Take your interactiveness with the book to a technological level by sharing "tweets" with others about what you're learning. If you send out tweets about a great tip you just learned, be sure to include the #techsavvyparent "hashtag." And if you don't know what a "tweet" or "hashtag" is, don't worry. You're in the right place to learn.

If your children are still young, familiarizing yourself with the topics included here will help you to get ahead of the curve. You can start processing some of these issues before they come knocking on your door. Keep in mind that technology will continue to change faster than a middle school girl's fashion tastes. There will be new challenges to face as your child grows and technology becomes a growing part of their life. In five years Facebook could be dead and gone, we may be making phone calls from our wrists, and every school could be outfitted with iPads, but you will at least have a framework to create a technologically balanced life as a family.

Controlling the Cell Phone Monster

"I can't get her attention anymore because she's always got that cell phone in her hand, texting nonstop." — One mom's words (through gritted teeth)

It's a recurring conversation I have with parents at conferences. I can't think of any other issue that sets parents off like mentioning texting and teenagers.[What was created to be a way to simplify communication has only made it more difficult for most families.]

While I understand and sympathize with the frustrations of parents concerning excessive teen texting, I don't think the blame can be placed solely on the shoulders of teenagers.

Think about it. When you were a kid and your parents bought you cotton candy at the fair, didn't you eat the whole thing at once? Of course. And when your mom gave you permission to stay up "a little later" when a friend was over to spend the night, didn't you instead try to stay awake the whole night? And surely you remember when your dad gave you a twenty as you were leaving the house. "Be sure to bring me the change," he would say. But did you remember to do that? Of course not. As teens, we were never good with limits if a clear boundary was not given. So why should we expect our children to do any better?

Maybe the issue has changed from a twenty-dollar bill on Friday night to sending/receiving more than 3,000 texts in a month's time, but the initial responsibility of educating always stops at the parent's feet. It's our job to be the ones to set limits and teach responsibility with our kids. We talked about playing in the street when they were wee little things. As they grew, we discussed issues of drugs and alcohol. Many parents have even gotten brave and broached

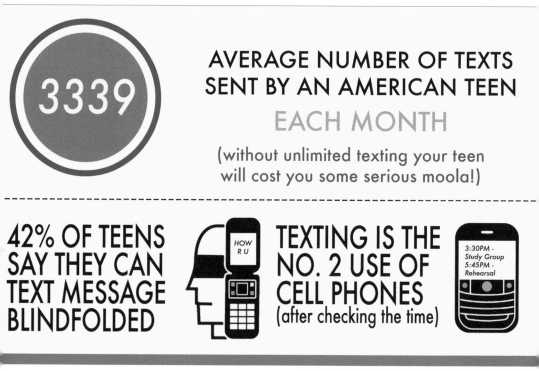

3339

AVERAGE NUMBER OF TEXTS SENT BY AN AMERICAN TEEN
EACH MONTH

(without unlimited texting your teen will cost you some serious moola!)

42% OF TEENS SAY THEY CAN TEXT MESSAGE BLINDFOLDED

HOW R U

TEXTING IS THE NO. 2 USE OF CELL PHONES
(after checking the time)

3:30PM - Study Group
5:45PM - Rehearsal

the difficult subject of sexual boundaries. But for whatever reason, when it comes to cell phones, most parents simply hand them over freely to their sweaty-handed, wide-eyed middle schoolers who are more than willing to use them to excess.

If getting face time with your teen has become nearly impossible because of the glowing apple or android in his hand, then it's time for you to take control of the cell phone monster. Stop being frustrated and start giving some clear boundaries for when and where the cell phone is to be used. Here are a few steps to establish good etiquette with the phone:

1. **Look Me in the Eyes.** Whenever your teen is talking to you face to face, the fingers need to pause. The person in front of him is always more important that the one at the other end of the line. It's going to take you training them to not answer their phone if they are in a conversation with an actual person in front of them. They should wait until the conversation is over, then excuse themselves to answer the phone.

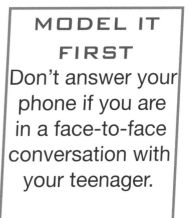

MODEL IT FIRST

Don't answer your phone if you are in a face-to-face conversation with your teenager.

This goes for you, too, Mom and Dad. Don't answer your phone if your teen is trying to have an actual conversation with you. Those moments can become fewer and fewer the older they get. Don't squander the chance to gain influence by answering your phone or responding to a text while he is talking.

I love being able to coach parents in helping them with their relationship with their teens. Once a distressed dad asked me to meet him for coffee to give him some pointers for better communication with his daughter. Several times while I was looking him in the eyes, speaking into his family situation, his phone rang. And he answered it. I finally put my hand on his phone as he was in motion to answer his third all-important, can't-wait-until-later, I-am-the-center-of-attention phone call. I said, "You asked me to be here. You asked for my help. But if you can't turn off your phone, I've got other places I can be." It may have sounded strong, but it was exactly what was wrong with his relationship between him and his daughter. No matter who is the one doing the talking, don't let technology be a barrier.

2. **Bedtime is for Sleeping.** The #1 location where teens get out of whack with texting is in the bedroom when they should be asleep. According to one study, the average heavy-texting teen is now losing one hour of sleep each night because of their inability to put down the phone. One teen texter said, "I'm afraid if I fall asleep, I might miss a text." Who does this kid think he is—the President of the United States? There is nothing in his life that can't wait until the morning. If anything, he is sabotaging his school focus for the next day.

> **MODEL IT FIRST**
> Unless you are the President, don't bring your cell phone to the table. Answer calls later.

Have him leave the phone on the counter at night to avoid temptation and to ensure a good night's sleep. Leaving the phone in a neutral room won't create an instant out-of-sight-out-of-mind situation, but it can help his mind to let go and relax at the end of the day.

3. **No Phones with the Pasta.** Research from CASA-Columbia shows that eating regular dinners together as a family can cut in half your teen's potential for at-risk behavior.[1] The key to the success of this practice is actually talking to one another during the meal. That can't happen if one of you is texting.

Teaching your teen to set aside technology for just a few minutes to talk at dinner will also help them to be intentional about this prac-

Teen Txtn & Drvn Don't Mix

5 sec. Amount of time a driver looks down when sending a text while driving

That is like driving 55MPH the length of a football field without looking up!

FOOTBALL FOOTBALL

80% of teens say someone has warned them of texting/driving.

40% of teens continue to text/drive anyway.

24% of of all accidents involve cell phone distrations.

Source: VTTI 2009, University of Utah 2009, Seventeen Magazine 2010, National Highway Traffic Safety Administration 2011

tice in public settings. When I meet colleagues for lunch, I make a point to put my phone on silent and set it face down on the table. I typically wait until they sit down to do this so they can see it. It's almost comical when they sheepishly look at me, then reach down to turn off their phones as well.

4. **Hands at Ten and Two.** If your teenager is old enough to drive alone, you definitely need to talk about never ever, ever, ever texting while driving. I'm guessing you will have a conversation with your teen about drinking and driving, but checking your phone has the equivalent distraction level of driving while legally drunk. Almost all teens say that their school has done a program about texting and driving. Still more than 1 in 4 admit to doing it. Their lives are too important to be put at risk for a text or phone call.

TEEN SEX & TECH FACTS

 39% of both teen guys and girls have sent

SEXUALLY SUGGESTIVE TEXT MESSAGES

48% of teens say they have received this type message

66% of the girls **&** **60%** of the boys

sent these messages to be "flirty" or "fun."

Girls who felt pressure from a guy to send sexual messages.	Girls who sent sexual messages to a guy they wanted to date or "hook up" with.	Girls who sent sexual messages to try and feel "sexy" or more attractive.
51%	**21%**	**34%**

Source: Sex & Tech, The National Campaign to Prevent Teen and Unplanned Pregnancy, (c) 2010

A Harris Interactive study asked teens about their feelings and actions when it comes to texting and driving. More than 80% of teens said that someone had talked to them about texting while driving. The same percentage agreed that it was a dangerous thing to do, but more than 30% of those same teens said that they do it.

As your teen is leaving the house with keys in hand, a good practice is to say once again, "Buckle up and no texting." Even if you say it every time, it can't be enough—it shows them you care about their safety.

5. **Data for Dollars.** Children need to understand that cell phones are expensive, and their use is a privilege rather than a right guaranteed by the Constitution. To give a teenager a phone with no expectation of financial obligation fails to teach them gratitude or responsibility. It is reasonable to put a limit on what you'll pay each month for a phone, then let the rest fall to them. For instance, you can put a limit on the number of texts. Anything over is ten cents each. Or if they exceed the data allowed on your family plan, they should pay the overage each month.

Flirting with the Phone

Loose restrictions and lack of guidance concerning their phones has created another unforeseen problem. For parents the camera can be a nightmare, but for teens it all seems innocent enough. Just point. Click. Shoot. Another instant picture via a cell phone. Tens of thousands of teens use their phones every day to send photos to friends. Most of the time the photos are innocuous—teens hanging out with friends, acting goofy in the halls at schools, or a lucky sighting of a celebrity. But a growing number of teens are redefining the game of flirting with a cell phone.

It's no longer enough to send a text message that reads, "Wanna go out? Just U & me." Now the invitation is accompanied by a teaser

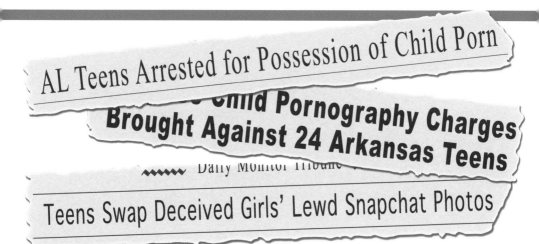

photo sent to the prospect. Far from a fringe behavior, this very forward (and visual) form of communication is now becoming common practice among both females and males. The Sex & Tech Survey revealed some startling trends with teens and their phones: 39% of all teens say they have sent or posted a sexually suggestive message, 71% of girls and 67% of guys said they sent the message to a boyfriend/girlfriend.[2]

There seems to be a corresponding link between internet usage and risky behavior among teens. As more and more teens use the internet as their primary community, their usage seems to get increasingly sexual. Teens start with making sexual remarks to friends online. The habit progresses to communicating with strangers. Posting provocative photos on their Facebook/Tumblr profiles soon follows. Now, one-on-one communication with photos that bare all is the rising trend: **20% of all teens say they have sent/posted nude or semi-nude pictures or videos of themselves**, 51% of girls said they felt pressure from a boyfriend to do so.

In 2010, 24 middle and high school students in Utah were arrested for taking and swapping nude photos of themselves. A similar case in Alabama involved four middle schoolers. The same thing has happened in California, Arkansas, Florida, and Ohio.

So far it has been difficult to find any legal way to prevent the practice. In Alabama, teens were arrested for "possession of materials harmful to a minor." Similarly, teens in Arkansas were charged with distribution of child pornography. The materials in question were pictures of themselves.

Girls have become more sexually aggressive to keep up with their male counterparts. When asked why they sent sexually suggestive pictures or videos...

- **66%** - TO BE "FUN OR FLIRTY" WITH A GUY.
- **52%** - TO GIVE A "SEXY PRESENT" TO THEIR BOYFRIEND.
- **30%** - IN HOPES OF GETTING A DATE OR HOOKING UP WITH A GUY.

An Engaged Response to Photo Flirting

As you read this, maybe your gut reaction is to take away your teen's cell phone or sit your child down for a little questioning under the interrogation lamp. You and I both know this is a course of action that will lead to no good. Don't get me wrong. You must respond. But respond in a way that helps your teen make well thought out choices. Here are a few situations to talk about in regard to purity and the cell phone.

1. **"Everything you do is part of your ongoing image."** As a parent you have a responsibility to teach your teens healthy boundaries for dating. Talk to them about using discernment in what they say and do with a prospective date. Help them see that every day they are creating an image (reputation) for others to see who they are as a person.

2. **"Once you send it, it's anybody's business."** This is particularly true for younger teens. Make sure your teen understands that if they send a photo to someone else, it can then be distributed to any number of other people. They no longer have control over who sees their picture. Furthermore, more than 40% of teens say they have seen a sexually explicit text that was meant for someone else. And there is virtually no way to stop it.

3. **"Present actions can have long-term consequences."** Both sexes feel emboldened by this new technology and freedom. They like the idea that they can be the talk of the school for a few minutes. According to a UCLA study, today's teens are more motivated by immediate fame than by planning for their future by making healthy choices today.[3] This kind of attitude fuels the need for attention that phone flirting can garner someone.

4. **"Your faith is both a safety net and a compass."** In Ephesians 5:3, Paul says there should not be "even a hint of sexual immorality" in our lives. Ask your teen how they deal with pressures like these from friends who might suggest it. Talk about God's design for sexuality and the freedom that comes from living within His boundaries. Ask your teen, "How can I help you to live within God's plan for freedom?" Provide a safe environment at home so they know they can talk to you if they ever feel pressured to take part in this kind of activity.

As other issues come up, don't hesitate to jump in and address them with your teen. After you talk it over, be sure you stay connected by putting it in writing. There is a sample **Cell Phone Contract** in the back of the book for you to use. Having a contract will insure that you and your teen are on the same page and make dealing with poor behavior easier. The Cell Phone Monster doesn't have to rule your home and destroy your family time. But to have balance in your family will require you to be the one to set the boundaries.

Got a Teen Texting Addict in Your Home?

Occasionally at the grocery store, I hear little voices calling out to me from the candy aisle. Like a recovering candy addict, I try to show restraint and avoid the section altogether. But on the rare occasion that I venture down the forbidden aisle, I can always hear them calling out to me. Those tiny multi-colored bears in the five-pound resealable bag. Once I reach for the bag, its game over for me. Gummy bears are my weakness.

I can sit and watch television with the giant bag of gelatin sweets in my lap, eating one after another after another. Before I realize what has happened, still buzzing with a sugar rush, I throw back more gummy bears than I care to admit. It's really quite embarrassing.

Would you believe it if I told you that your teen's text-messaging habit might be every bit as addictive? No, I'm not suggesting the wasted-over-a-toilet-hating-yourself kind of addiction. It's the kind of addiction where you lose track of time, become detached from those around you, and experience a drug-like happiness. Sound like anyone you might know?

According to Dr. Gary Small, author of *iBrain: Surviving the Technological Alteration of the Modern Mind,* a teen who habitually texts receives a rush in their brain. He reports that neuroimaging studies show that **when a teen sends and receives texts, the same part of their brain lights up as an addict's using heroin.** There is a release of dopamine in their system that causes a feeling of pleasure or reward.[1]

I don't recommend telling your daughter, "You're acting like a crack addict with that phone," the next time you see her texting. That will get you nothing more than a well deserved rolled-eyes, slammed-door response. That's not the point of the study. It simply shows that there is a correlation between the pleasure part of the brain and excessive texting, and that it in can lead to the feelings and behaviors of addiction.

Knowing the Signs

The American Journal of Psychiatry states that excessive emailing and texting may be part of a compulsive-impulsive spectrum disorder and a form of addiction. Here is a list of symptoms from the AJP to discern if your teen has a problem:

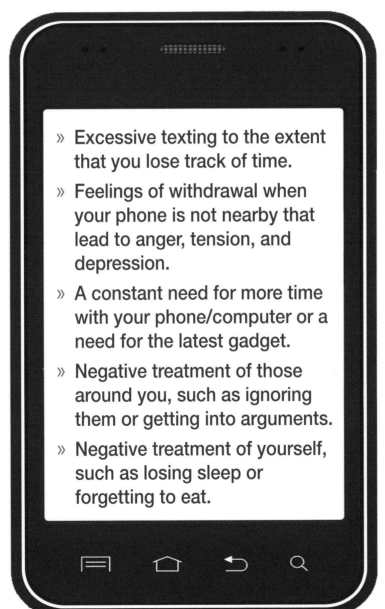

» Excessive texting to the extent that you lose track of time.

» Feelings of withdrawal when your phone is not nearby that lead to anger, tension, and depression.

» A constant need for more time with your phone/computer or a need for the latest gadget.

» Negative treatment of those around you, such as ignoring them or getting into arguments.

» Negative treatment of yourself, such as losing sleep or forgetting to eat.

The Healthy Disconnect

Looking at the list from the previous page, if you are like most parents of a texting teen, you're probably thinking, "That exactly describes my child! My teenager's picture could be right next to that list." Take a deep breath. It's not time to strap your teen down and sign them up for shock therapy. There are probably some logical reasons why your teen is an obsessive texter.

Many teens struggle with excessive texting because they feel an obligation to be "on" for their friends. This, of course, is an unhealthy view of friendship where your teen feels like she owes her friends something or can somehow meet all of her friends needs. It can be easy for her to lose her own identity in the process. Being a part of a community (peer group) is one of the core values of teenagers, but there has to be a time for her to shut down and be alone.

Disconnecting from the phone for a period of time each day gives her a chance to decompress and to set aside the various conversations on her phone. It also gives her brain time to process everything she has seen on that tiny screen throughout the day or simply to have a few minutes to think her own thoughts. More importantly,

Teaching Your Teen Rhythms

Life is a series of rhythms. Imagine each of the areas of life like a rhythmic wave. There are times you are fully engaged and "all on." There are other times you set things aside to rest or recharge. You've learned that you can't do all things all of the time.

it just might give the two of you a chance to connect.

Those intentional screen-free moments in our home have become some of the best bonding times for our family. Our kids' phones and iPods still illuminate their faces for much of the day, but the designated times in the evening when all screens are turned off has allowed us to see each others' faces and to make shared memories in the process.

Setting the Boundaries

In the end, you're going to have to be the parent when it comes to unplugging. You can't expect your teen to be the one to muster a fully-functioning self-discipline routine overnight. This is especially true if you've treated texting like giving a gummy bear addict free reign of the candy aisle. This doesn't mean you have to be heavy-handed or mean. We're talking about reasonable expectations. Here are a few to start with:

1. **Hour-of-Day Restrictions.** This could mean no texting after 9PM or before 8AM. You determine the hours based on your teen's schedule.

For your teenager, they may have the rhythm of school, rhythm of family, rhythm of the spirit, and yes, rhythm of technology. Help them see that when you ask them to "unplug" for the night or a weekend, it isn't punishment. You are trying to teach them natural rhythms of life. Scripture calls this time a Sabbath where we can focus on God and resting.

2. **School is for School.** Definitely no texting during school hours. This is also a big temptation for cheating among students. Find out your child's school policy concerning cell phones and make sure your teen observes it. A nice bonus is this can help cut down on the gossip and drama that happens at school.

3. **Limit the Number of Texts.** The average texting teen now sends over 3,000 texts a month. Consider putting a cap on the maximum amount of texts that can be sent/received each month. Anything over that amount she has to pay for. The goal here isn't necessarily to limit text. It is to teach moderation in all things.

4. **Put the Phone in a Public Place.** At the end of the day, everyone's phones should go on the counter to avoid the temptation to text at night and thus lose sleep. This isn't about trust. It's about helping your teenager understand the rhythm concept. If Solomon lived today, he might say, "There is a time to text, and a time to sleep."

5. **Homework Comes First.** Have her put the cell phone out of sight while doing homework. She'll be able to focus and finish faster. Don't use the phone's calculator or clock features as an excuse to keep it nearby, otherwise the magnet of Instagram and Facebook will suck her in when she should be studying.

Obviously, this is not a complete list of suggestions. These are but a few ideas to consider. You've still got to use discernment to know what is best for your child, depending on how extreme the texting situation. In order to get both of you on the same page, consider using a Cell Phone Contract. Just like the piece of paper you had to sign before walking out of the phone store, have your teen sign one that states your expectations as well as the recourse for breached boundaries. After you each sign it, give her a copy to keep. This shows her that you are raising the bar of responsibility in her life and that having a cell phone is a privilege to be exercised wisely.

Using the Phone to Connect with Your Teen

Admit it—when you first think of calling your teen on her cell phone, it's not to chat. My guess is that more often it's to make sure she is where she is supposed to be, to nag her about chores left undone, or to remind her when to be home. In short, as much as we want to say that we like our teens having cell phones because it "makes them safe," the reality is we primarily use the device as

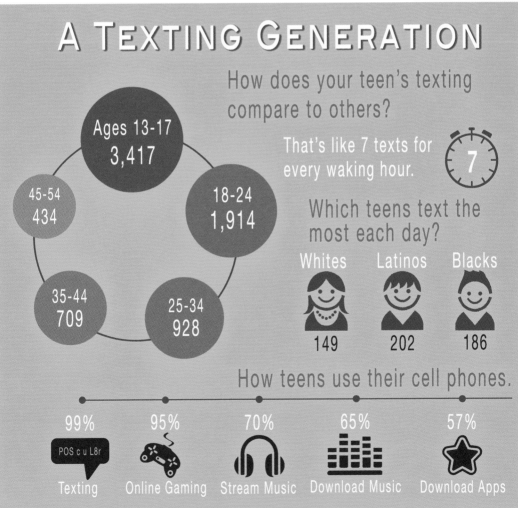

A TEXTING GENERATION

How does your teen's texting compare to others?

Ages 13-17
3,417

That's like 7 texts for every waking hour.
7

45-54
434

18-24
1,914

Which teens text the most each day?

Whites   Latinos   Blacks

149   202   186

35-44
709

25-34
928

How teens use their cell phones.

99%   95%   70%   65%   57%

POS c u L8r
Texting   Online Gaming   Stream Music   Download Music   Download Apps

Source: "New Mobile Obsession: US Teens Triple Data Usage," blog.nielson.com, 2011.

another way to keep tabs on their behavior.

When your number pops up on your daughter's phone, can you see why her first response is to snarl the same way you do when a telemarketer calls during dinner? Her first thought is, "What did I do now?" or "What does she want me to do now?" But what if instead of your daughter dreading your call, you used the cell phone to improve your relationship with your teen?

Recent research shows that using a cell phone to contact your teen can create a better relationship between the two of you. This research from Robert Weisskirch from California State University shows that teenagers report a higher degree of stress and conflict with their parents when their parents call their cell phone to monitor them. On the other hand, teens who call their parents for advice or support in a social situation reported a more supportive and encouraging relationship with their parents.[2]

This could mean that teens who are more likely to call their parents for advice do so because they already enjoy a trusting relationship with their parents. Likewise, parents who use the cell phone to nag their teens may already have a negative relationship with them. Either way, the study isn't trying to show that a cell phone is the silver bullet that will fix everything between you and your teen. However, it can make things worse if you don't use it with proper boundaries yourself.

Letting Them Fail on Their Own

If you have asked your teen to be at a certain place or she has told you she will be there, then you trust she will be there. If she says she will do something, you trust she will do it. Unless she has given you reason not to trust her actions, you are able treat her like the responsible person she has proven to be.

Some parents use the cell phone as a way of being their teen's personal secretary or pseudo life-coach. Reminding your teen about a doctor's appointment you scheduled for him is one thing, but reminding your sixteen year old to finish a school project or get to a church youth group on time every week is going overboard. Whether sink or swim, these small tasks need to fall squarely on his shoulders. In part, your teen will learn a greater sense of responsibility from having to remember his own "to do" list as opposed to you sending a constant stream of text message reminders. This may mean he forgets to do a few things—things he may have to pay the consequences for later. Even so, it is all part of an important learning process for him. Those lessons will be much more valuable to him in the long run than your reminders could ever be.

TWEET IT
Don't use the phone just to "check up" on your teen. Use it to send them an encouraging text & tell them why u love them.
#techsavvyparent

Texting a Happy Teen

There are a number of ways you can use your calls and messages to enhance your relationship with your teen. Here are a few ways to effectively use the cell phone to connect with your teen:

Send an encouraging text on the days he has a "big event" such as a major test, school presentation, or sport tryouts. Your word of encouragement can serve as a reminder without being blatant or nagging such as, "Thinking about you today during your tryouts. Can't wait to hear how it went."

Text her an inspirational quote or picture you saw that reminds you of her. No need to send an explanation or long message. Short and sweet makes the point. The key here is occasionally.

Give your teen a call if you are going to be late or away from home when you normally would be there. You expect the same.

When she is gone on a group trip for several days, **give her one day without hearing from you.** It's okay to call the second day. Giving some space can be good for independence, but calling on day two lets her know you're still in the picture.

Let your teen use you as her "out" in a socially or morally awkward situation. You can check in on her if it's a first date, school dance, sleepover, etc. A quick, "Everything okay?" is all it takes. If she feels uncomfortable being there, she can always say, "My dad just sent me a text; he needs me to come home."

> ## MODEL IT
> ## FIRST
> Give your teen a call if you will be unusually late. You expect the same of them.

The next time you feel an urge to call or send a text to your teen, stop and ask yourself what your motivation might be. Calling your teen out of concern or texting to give an encouraging word can go a long way to showing you care about their everyday issues. On the other hand, if you never get a text or a callback, you could be contacting too often or need to look for time for a face-to-face conversation.

You'll never be able to text as quickly as your teenager. Perhaps it is the youthful nimbleness of their fingers, but chances are your teen can send an entire text before you can find the keys to spell your name. Nonetheless, if you want to raise your "cool factor" a bit, try sending them a message with some texting lingo. They'll roll their eyes at it, but love you all the same. Here are a few to start with.

TOY RN (Thinking of you right now)
Im prayN 4 U 2day (I'm praying for you today)
DYK w@ I luv bout U? (Do you know what I love about you?)
@ *$$s. wnt a trEt (At Starbucks. Want a treat?)

Setting iPhone and iPod Parental Controls

A couple walked up to me with pained and sheepish looks on their faces. "We had to take our 12 year old's iPod away because he was looking at pornography."

I asked what I thought was an obvious question. "Had you already explained proper boundaries to him and that this was not allowed?" Their response was common. "We didn't even know you could get on the internet with that thing."

Knowing what the iPod (or any device) can and can't do is a parent's job BEFORE giving it to a child. Even a cursory investigation would make access to the internet easy to spot. Secondly, there should always be a conversation to explain proper boundaries and behavior when giving a new privilege to your child. But enough with the scolding. Let's get to the real issue.

Inappropriate use of the iPod Touch or iPhone is a big issue with teens and tweens who own them. Though an obvious area of abuse is viewing pornography on adult websites, other issues may include viewing inappropriate YouTube videos, downloading "explicit" songs, or downloading unauthorized apps or games. If your child's iDevice is "wide open"—meaning all the functions are turned on—they will be more susceptible to cyberbullying, more likely to be accidently exposed to pornography, more likely to be contacted by strangers, and more likely to set poor social boundaries.

While all of these issues should be covered in a conversation with your child before giving them the device, there is an additional step you can take to lessen the temptation or exposure—parental controls (cue ominous music). Take a deep breath. It's really not as bad as you may think. The good news is you don't have to be a techno geek to do this. We'll walk through it together.

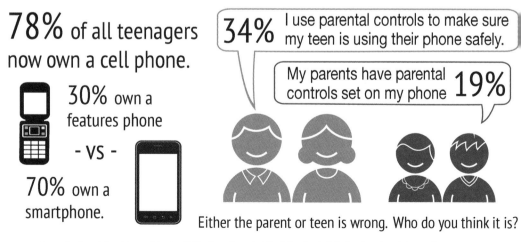

78% of all teenagers now own a cell phone.

30% own a features phone

- vs -

70% own a smartphone.

34% I use parental controls to make sure my teen is using their phone safely.

My parents have parental controls set on my phone **19%**

Either the parent or teen is wrong. Who do you think it is?

Resource: Pew Research Center's Internet & American Life Teen/Parent Survey, Apr. 2001.; Nielson, Ring the Bells: More Smartphones in Students' Hands, Nov. 2013.

Apple has done an excellent job of making the parental controls easy to set up. With a few simple steps you can breathe a little easier that your child can enjoy safe and appropriate usage of his iDevice. If you've got the iPod or phone with you now and are ready to set those controls, then keep reading. If not, put down your coffee and go grab the iPod/iPhone. Surely, you agree that it's pointless to learn how to set the controls unless you are going to do it. After all, that's why you're reading this in the first place. For each step, I'm going to walk through a series of screenshots so you can follow along.

●●●●○ AT&T 📶	9:47 PM	🔋 85% 🔋

Settings

📶	Wi-Fi	Housman >
✱	Bluetooth	On >
⦾	Cellular	>
⊘	Personal Hotspot	Off >
🔲	Notification Center	>
🔳	Control Center	>
🌙	Do Not Disturb	>
⊚	General	>
🔊	Sounds	>
✴	Wallpapers & Brightness	>

1. STEP ONE:

Select the Settings icon. Unless you've moved it, it is located in the top left-hand corner of the first screen. Most of the changes to your iPod, iPhone, or iPad start from the **Settings Screen**. You'll want to spend some time here getting familiar with the changes you can make. Take a minute to scroll up and down to see what is here. However, the area of most concern to you now is the General Tab.

Scroll down until you see the **General Tab**. Select by touching.

This screen shows you general information about your iDevice such as the wireless network you are on or the software version your iPod or iPhone is running. The **About Tab** is full of strings of numbers that can look confusing, but if you ever need to call Technical Support or have your device worked on you'll need the information here. Otherwise don't worry about it. What you are really looking for here is the **Restrictions Tab** at the bottom. Scroll down until you see it, then touch to go to the next screen.

2. STEP TWO:
After selecting the Restrictions tab you will need to enter your four digit **Passcode**. If you don't have one, you can create one now. Be sure to make your Passcode something you will remember. Forgetting it can put you in a difficult position in the future.

The only way to reset your restrictions if you forget your Passcode is to completely erase your phone and start from scratch.

●●●●○ AT&T 📶	11:10 AM	⚹ 86% 🔋
	Enter Passcode	Cancel

Enter your Restrictions Passcode

— — — —

1	2 ABC	3 DEF
4 GHI	5 JKL	6 MNO
7 PQRS	8 TUV	9 WXYZ
	0	⊗

3. STEP THREE:
Once you type in your Passcode, the Restriction Screen will come on. The bulk of the changes you'll want to make are on this screen. Most of these should be self-explanatory, but we'll walk through a few of the more important ones together.

Function "ON"

Function "OFF"

Apple devices come out of the box with all of their functions turned on. Unfortunately, not all of those functions are good for younger children or unguarded teens.

LIVING IN THE APPMOSPHERE

Guess what is on your teen's phone or iPod. Here are the top downloaded apps among teenagers.

Tumblr
Microblogging app more popular with teens than Facebook. Poor filters.

Vine
Allows you to create and send 8 second videos. Poor filters & inappropriate content.

Twitter
Teens have been migrating to this quick posting site.

kik messenger
The most popular messenging app among teens. Alias identities make for poor accountability.

Instagram
Most popular photo posting app with teens. Can set limits on who can see your photos.

Omegle
Thinking of texting & roulette combined. Tagline is "text with strangers." Beware!

Snapchat
This app lets you send photos to friends with a viewing limit. Easy means of sexting for teens.

Pheed
Pulls all of your social media outlets together into one app.

Ask.fm
Users post & answer questions. There are no limits on the types of questions asked.

A function is turned on when the slider is green and it is disabled when it is in gray.

Safari is the native internet browser for iDevices. If you are concerned about your child having access to the Internet, then slide Safari to OFF. **Facetime** is used for video chatting. If your child isn't mature enough to use this responsibly, slide it to OFF as well. You can always turn it back on later.

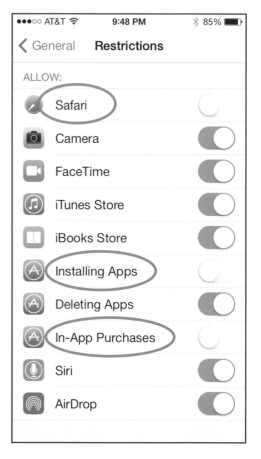

Installing Apps allows the user to access the Apple App Store and download new apps. This can be dangerous for younger children that may not be able to judge whether or not a particular app is appropriate. It's best to turn this function OFF in the beginning and let your child earn this privilege.

If Installing Apps is turned ON, all your child needs to download an app is the iTunes account password. Many of the apps are free, but not all. You don't want

Candy Crush Saga is a wildly popular game app. It is also the highest grossing app of all time even though it is a "freemium" app. Freemium games are initially free. Candy Crush Saga makes its money through in-app purchases such as extra lives, extra moves, and power ups. The game grosses more than $850,000 each day; translating into serious real world money.

‹ General   Restrictions

ALLOWED CONTENT:

Ratings For	United States >
Music & Podcasts	Clean >
Movies	All >
TV Shows	TV-14 >
Books	All >
Apps	All >
Siri	All >
Websites	All >
Require Password	15 minutes >

Require password for purchases.

PRIVACY:

your child or teen to run up a credit card bill by downloading the latest Call of Duty or Grand Theft Auto. The same goes for In-App Purchases.

Another restriction function is the **In-App Purchases**. Slide this to OFF to keep anyone from purchasing items within apps such as virtual money or game "boosts." This is a big issue with kids who don't realize that money in games like Farmville or Temple Run is paid for with hard earned cash by means of your iTunes account. There is no good reason for this to be on.

4. **STEP FOUR:** Keep scrolling down the Restrictions screen and you will see the **Allowed Content Section.** Make note of the Music & Podcasts tab. When you select it, you will be taken to this screen. Setting it to CLEAN will disable those items that iTunes terms EXPLICIT. This only works for purchases made within the iTunes store, so any content that was physically placed on the computer will be up to you to monitor. To get back, select the Restriction button at the top.

You should now be back in the Allowed Content section. The next two steps will help you set restrictions on other types of media

WATCH OUT

The wrong App settings can leave you with a suprise credit card bill. Make sure you turn these OFF!

content. Selecting the Movies tab will allow you to set the ratings level for movies you'll allow to be downloaded. Again this only works for purchases made within the iTunes store. If you prefer not to allow movies, select Don't Allow Movies. To get back, select the Restriction button at the top.

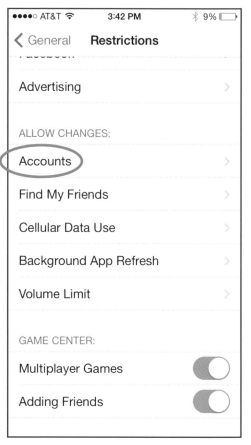

You should once again be back in the Allowed Content section. Selecting the TV Shows tab will allow you to set the ratings level for TV programs you'll allow to be downloaded. Again this only works for purchases made within the iTunes store. You are now finished. To exit the Restrictions, press the Home Button. It is the round button at the bottom of your phone.

5. STEP FIVE:

As you scroll down the screen, you will see the **Allow Changes Section**. If you slide this to OFF, you can keep anyone from setting up new email accounts on the iPod and restrict access to email. Whether or not you want your child to be able to get email on their iPod should depend on their age and maturity.

Getting Everyone on the Same Page

As a parent, keep in mind that the primary function of Parental Controls is not snooping, taking away control, or limiting fun. One of the core needs for teens is security. He may go on and on about how he wants independence and needs to "be his own man," but he is also looking to you to help provide a safe environment for him. When he was a baby, I'm guessing you covered the electrical outlets. It's also safe to assume you moved the Drain-O from under the sink so he wouldn't get into it. Your toddler wasn't looking to defy your authority when he took off running into the street. He didn't know that playing in the street was a bad choice for him. Parental controls are simply another step in the process of keeping your child safe now that he is a little older.

Assure your disconcerted teenager that these safeguards are not to provoke an issue of trust where he will with respond with, "Mom, why don't you trust me that I wouldn't do something like that?" As a parent, what I don't always trust is my own ability to keep my children safe. It is impossible to be on top of every website to avoid or know where the cultural land mines are going to be buried next. Nor do I trust my own ability to make consistent choices with their best interest in mind when I'm stressed out or tired. I'm sure you've experienced the frustration of having a demanding child who wants pizza for dinner for the third night in a row. With the collision of their whining and your exhaustion after a long day, suddenly pizza once again doesn't sound like a bad idea. The same thing happens with your child and their tech gadgets. Setting automatic parental controls help you to make the choice once, and then it's done.

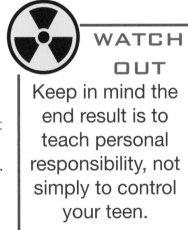

WATCH OUT

Keep in mind the end result is to teach personal responsibility, not simply to control your teen.

One last step in the process is to help your teen make wise choices even when you are not around. The end goal is a character of integrity and responsibility that your teen takes with them to college and beyond when you are no longer there to make hard choices for him.

There will come a day when temptations to compromise will be glaring him in the face and you won't be around. For instance, over a Christmas break I talked with a group of college freshmen about how they were enjoying their college experience. "What's been the most difficult transition for you in adjusting to college?" I expected learning to wake themselves up, getting to class on time, or maybe even trying to avoid the dreaded "freshmen 15." Instead, without missing a beat, they all agreed that no matter where they went in the dorm, it was impossible to get away from pornography.

Set your son up for success by building a solid foundation now. Part of doing this is agreeing together on what is appropriate and not appropriate when it comes to the iPod. An easy way to do this is an iPod or Cell Phone Contract. As an adult, you have a contract on your home, your car, and maybe even your job. A contract is a way of getting both parties on the same page with regards to expectations. A simple iPod/Cell phone Contract will help define what you desire of your child when it comes to iPod usage. As they get older, you can continue to revisit and adapt the contract to allow greater freedom.

Flip to the back of the book to the Resource Section. You'll find a sample contract you can copy or head over to www.360family.org and download one to use.

Video Game Violence and Moral Behavior

Saying that kids like video games would be a wild understatement. A whopping 97% of 12-17 year olds play video games, making it the most popular activity among teenagers.[1] On any given day 60% of teenagers will play a video game in their home. With $12 billion dollars in video games sales come concerns that the excessive violence in many of the games leads to aggressive behavior in those that play them.

Violent content in video games has been blamed for school shootings, bullying, poor grades, and violence toward women. The parental fear is obvious—if my son plays violent video games, he might become a social delinquent that beats up on 98-pound weaklings.

Over the past twenty years, there have been more than 85 scientific studies done to measure the effects video games have on the minds and actions of children and teens. The cumulative results of these studies are nearly unanimous. **In a nutshell, overwhelming evidence says "yes, video games have an adverse effect on developing minds."** To be fair, there have been a few studies that concluded children can play as much as they want because video games have no effect on them. But it must also be noted that those studies were largely funded by organizations from within the video game industry. This is akin to those studies from the 70s by the tobacco industry that concluded that "smoking tobacco has no addictive qualities."

What's Bad is Now Good?

The most startling effect that violent games have on kids was not increased aggression but rather a decrease in moral sensitivity. Basically, the longer a child plays violent games, the more desensitized he becomes to real life violence and to the hardships of others.

A 2004 study published in the Journal of Adolescence concluded that children who regularly play violent video games were less likely to feel bad when their friends were upset and more likely to feel it is okay to retaliate if someone hits them. They were also more likely to disagree with a statement such as, "When I am mean to someone, I generally feel bad about it later."

According to well-known pediatrician Dr. William Sears, the longer a child is exposed to video-game violence, it's as if the child develops an immunity to seeing the harshness of evil in the real world. "At a very young age, children learn to associate violence with plea-

Grand Theft Auto is the one of the top two best-selling franchises of all-time. The latest installment includes scenes of torture, sex acts, and lap dances from prostitutes. Total sales of the GTA franchise are $10 billion. Grand Theft Auto 5, Rockstar Games, ©2013. Xbox 360, ARR UBP

sure and excitement." There is an emotional rush that comes from playing the games. But the longer they play, the more difficult it is to feel that same rush. Dr. Sears goes on to say, "They build up an immunity to violence and therefore need higher levels of violence as 'booster shots.'"

Part of the moral confusion kids must navigate when playing violent video games is not simply that there is evil, but rather how you are to interact with the evil as a player. For decades, you could count on a predictable pattern in child's entertainment when it came to good versus evil. Whether it was Tubbs and Crocket fighting drug lords in the 80s, Buffy the Vampire Slayer ridding her town of the undead in the 90s, or more recently Anakin's slide to the dark side of the Force, you knew that good was going to win out in the end.

In many popular mass multiplayer games (MMP), players now play the game as the evil character. For instance in The Godfather II, you can play as an Italian gang enforcer roaming the streets killing anyone in your way. In Grand Theft Auto IV, your character is a released convict who now works as an auto thief. At different points

Problem Area	Type of Behavior in Past Year	Percentage of Boys Involved in Behavior	Percentage of M-Gamers	Percentage of Non M-Gamers
AGGRESSION AND BULLYING	Been in a physical fight	44.4%	51%	28%
	Hit or beat person	53.2%	60%	39%
	Took part in bullying a student	9.2%	10%	8%
DELINQUENT BEHAVIORS	Damaged property just for fun	18.6%	23%	10%
	Got in trouble with the police	4.9%	6%	2%
	Stole something from a store	10.5%	13%	6%
SCHOOL PROBLEMS	Got poor grades	31.6%	35%	23%
	Skipped school without excuse	11.2%	13%	8%
	Got into trouble with teacher	52.9%	60%	39%
	Got suspended from school	20.1%	22%	15%

Teenage Guys' Problem Behavior & M-Rated Video Games

Problem Area	Type of Behavior in Past Year	Percentage of Girls Involved in Behavior	Percentage of M-Gamers	Percentage of Non M-Gamers
AGGRESSION AND BULLYING	Been in a physical fight	20.0%	40%	14%
	Hit or beat person	34.5%	49%	29%
	Took part in bullying a student	4.4%	6%	4%
DELINQUENT BEHAVIORS	Damaged property just for fun	7.9%	15%	5%
	Got in trouble with the police	1.8%	2%	2%
	Stole something from a store	9.8%	14%	8%
SCHOOL PROBLEMS	Got poor grades	23.7%	37%	20%
	Skipped school without excuse	10.8%	20%	7%
	Got into trouble with teacher	35.5%	49%	31%
	Got suspended from school	8.4%	16%	5%

Teenage Girls' Problem Behavior & M-Rated Video Games

in the game, your job is to shoot at and outrun the police, visit strip bars, and terrorize citizens with your car in hopes of getting the high score. Instead of violence, sexism, or racism being punished, these types of behavior are rewarded with "power-ups," extra lives, and bonus scores in many of the games.

Escapism with No Escape

The pleasure of media viewing is that it allows you to unplug from the real world and to escape to a fantasy world for a few minutes. When my brother and I were kids, we used to watch wrestling every Saturday morning. Afterwards we would pretend to be "Macho Man" Randy Savage and Jerry "The King" Lawler. Our mother would watch with heightened tension as we would sling each other into our couch which served as our turnbuckle. Even though we would pretend to punch and clothesline one another, there was never any real harm done. Unfortunately, the same cannot be said of kids who regularly play violent video games. What is seen on the screen can bleed over into real life attitudes.

⚟))) WHAT TEENS SAY

Have you ever bought or received an "M" rated game.

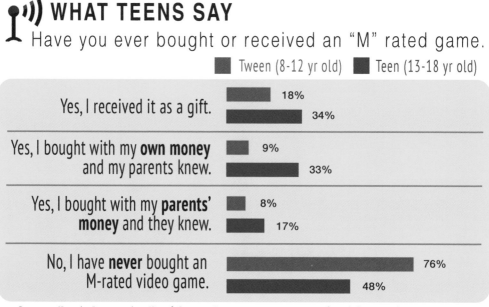

Tween (8-12 yr old)   Teen (13-18 yr old)

	Tween	Teen
Yes, I received it as a gift.	18%	34%
Yes, I bought with my **own money** and my parents knew.	9%	33%
Yes, I bought with my **parents' money** and they knew.	8%	17%
No, I have **never** bought an M-rated video game.	76%	48%

Source: Harris Interactive YouthQuery, Jan. 17-23, 2007. www.harrisinteractive.com

In Hitman: Absolution, you play as an assassin (Agent 47). The latest installment includes scenes of strangulation, snorting cocaine, and a visit to a strip club. The Hitman franchise has sold more than 10 million copies.
Hitmans: Absolution, IO Interactive, ©2012, Xbox 360, ARR UBP.

The lifelike graphics and realism in the story line puts the player close to the action. Newer game controllers bring gameplay directly into your hands. The Wii controller and nunchuk allow you to move the controller to simulate running, punching, stabbing, etc. The camera on the Xbox Kinect actually watches your whole body movement and reacts on screen as you shoot, maim, slap, or do other destructive behavior. If you're playing a game of table tennis, waving your arms like you have a paddle, the Kinect can be good family fun. But if you're playing an excessive amount of a game in which you wave your arms like you are wielding a chainsaw as the street gang on the screen bleeds out, then studies say it is just too real for the typical teen brain to differentiate.

Among all forms of media, video game violence is the only one associated with a lower empathy level in kids. A 2004 study from the University of Toledo examined responses of 150 fourth and fifth graders to different media stimulus. **Violent video games were the only stimuli that lowered empathy**—the ability of a person to understand the feelings of another person. In other

86% of the time children receive their parents' permission before purchasing a video game.

words, these types of games were the one type of media that causes a child to lose the ability to feel bad about another person's pain or circumstances.

Another study showed that kids who played violent games the longest were more likely to agree with the statement, "People with guns or knives are cool," and "Parents should tell their kids to fight if they have to." This takes the effect even further. Children don't merely lose the ability to feel bad, they begin to approve of violence. We are talking about an actual change in the child's moral worldview (belief system). University of Michigan researcher Brad Bushman says, "Video games increase aggressive thought and angry feelings. They increase arousal levels such as heart rate and blood pressure. They increase aggressive behavior and they decrease helping behavior."[2]

In the eye-opening book, *Grand Theft Childhood: The Surprising Truth about Violent Video Games and What Parents Can Do*, researchers carried out an interesting study. The authors, Drs. Lawrence Kutner and Cheryl Olsen examined all areas of life among two groups of teens—those who regularly played violent games and those who did not.

In every area of teen life, unhealthy behavior was greater among those teens who regularly played violent video games. One argument by those who think all of this is silliness is, "Well, those are kids who were predisposed to bad behavior by their upbringing or personality." This could be true were it not for the fact that in many of the

64% of parents believe video games are are a positive part of their children's lives.

studies kids were randomly chosen to play either violent or non-violent games. In each case the kids that played the violent games showed an adverse effect.

"It's Really No Big Deal"

Even though study after study has concluded that video game violence does has a temporal effect on adolescent decision making and aggression, there are still critics who disagree. In a recent post on the gaming website www.Kotaku.com, a long-time GameStop employee wrote a scathing article about the sheer number of parents buying Grand Theft Auto V for their 9-12 year olds. He talks about nine year olds running out of the store waving their GTA V in the air with their hapless parents following behind.

What was interesting was the response to the article from other gamers—particularly dads. Here are a few of the comments from dads of teens/tweens.

*"I would personally have no problem playing GTA V with my twelve year old daughter. It completely **changes the context for them emotionally** when you play with them."*

*"I'd much rather buy my kid GTA and have a talk with them and trust that I've raised them right than to **deny them every bit of modern enjoyment.**"*

*"I don't see what the big deal is. There is not that much profanity and violence. There's really **nothing here that teenagers don't see every day in their life.**"*

*"Each child is different and will perceive experiences in different ways; part of being a parent is knowing **how to shape those experiences in a positive way.**"*

This was just a sampling of the same attitude from dads repeated over and over again on the website. There are some key phases these dads used that I hope you caught. One, games have an emotional context. Two, as parents, we help shape what they experience in a positive way. Three, the content of video games is just like real teenage life.

DO "M" RATED GAMES HIT THE MARK?

Read through the following list of activities you can experience in the GTA V video game. Rate each statement as either "yes" or "no" based on the following criteria:

1. Does the game invoke a good emotional context?
2. Does the game create a positive experience?
3. Does the game reflect what the typical teen will experience in their world?

	Torture a man by waterboarding.	YES	NO
	Pull out a man's teeth with pliers.	YES	NO
	Murder a pedestrian for his money.	YES	NO
	Crush a man's skull with your foot.	YES	NO
	Have sex with a prostitute in an alley.	YES	NO
	Stuff money into a stripper's G-string.	YES	NO
	Video record a celebrity having anal sex.	YES	NO
	Drink while high speed driving.	YES	NO
	Snort cocaine and smoke marijuana.	YES	NO
	Steal, hijack, and destroy vehicles.	YES	NO

You Be the One

As a parent, it is always a temptation to blame something else for our kids' behavior. We blame too much TV for childhood obesity, teachers for failing grades, and video game violence for childhood aggression. The reality is that outside factors can contribute to a poor childhood experience, but none of these takes us off the hook as parents.

More than likely, no one else but you is going to monitor your child in regards to what TV shows they watch, how much time they surf the web, or the types of video games they play. It's going to come down to you and how much you are willing to invest in how and how much they use video games. Here are some suggested guidelines for you to consider.

1. **Create a "No Go" List.** This is a list of non-negotiables for video game use, such as no TV or video-game playing in a bedroom, no T-rated video games or above without your parent's consent and presence in the room, and no video games before homework. Depending on your child's maturity and learning level, you may even add to the list no video games of any kind on school nights. As much as they will complain about it, they will survive without a daily dose of Call of Duty: Special Ops. This could apply to hand-held video games on a DS, too.

2. **Offer Alternatives to Release Aggression.** Teenagers need to have a way to release aggression and to be active each day. Getting your kids involved in activities such as sports, gymnastics, paintball, or target practice are ways to get exercise and experience a healthy dose of risk. Social clubs such as 4H, Boy Scouts, Girl Scouts, and church youth groups provide an outlet for activity and interaction. If your child has a special talent such as horseback riding or acting, nurture those disciplines that will reward them and build self-esteem throughout their lifetime.

3. **Monitor the Screen.** Just as you would watch a controversial TV program or movie with your child and discuss it with them, you should do the same with video games. Many of the role-playing games are built around a story line that unfolds as the game is played. Also, some of the more violent games start off mild then build in intensity the further you get into the game. Having the video system in a family room will allow you to see what is happening at all times. You can also use YouTube to preview game play before deciding to purchase a game.

4. **Establish a Video Game Bank.** Life is best lived when done within healthy boundaries and moderation. You can help instill personal responsibility in other areas of life by starting in small areas such as video games. Give your child a set amount of time per week or per day that he/she can play video games. Once they withdraw all of their time out of the "bank," the play time is over. This is an easy win for all of you because they get to play video games (which is what they want), and you know there is a time cutoff (which is what you want). This worked well with both of our kids when they were 5-9 years old and just starting to play video games.

Banning all video games runs the risk of you showing little regard for his need for "guy time." Find a healthy balance for both video games and time without the screens.

5. **Encourage Group Games.** Multiplayer video game play is the number one activity for middle school boys. Make sure some of your child's time playing games is done in a group. This causes your child to socially interact with others while learning concepts such as teamwork, patience, cooperation, and celebration. You should also mention to him that the same standards for your home apply when he is visiting someone else's home.

6. **Evaluate the Game Rating.** The Entertainment Software Rating Board (ESRB) was created to rate video games and to create a standard age appropriateness. They do a good job in rating the games and explaining their rationale, but it is still a subjective process. Your job is to read the rating for the games you buy for your kids and to understand the content. We'll cover all of the ratings explanations in the next chapter.

Moderation in Everything

Don't misunderstand the real message of this chapter. I am not making an argument that video games or video game makers are all bad. Neither am I saying you shouldn't ever play certain types of games. I'm merely trying to give an honest assessment of the research done so far. It is up to you as a parent to decide how you will use the information to better lead your family.

Keep in mind that the majority of the studies are not arguing against violent video games but rather EXCESS PLAY. Each year the amount of time children spend playing video games goes up. **The average teen boy now spends 97 minutes a day playing video games.** Perhaps a balance for your family could be that if your son is going to play a game such as Halo or Modern Warfare, he has to play with you in the room and in strict moderation. And if you play together, use it as a teachable time by debriefing after gameplay. If the game tells a story, use it the same way you would a movie. Let there be a few moments of quietness after gameplay to talk about what you experienced and saw in the video. No matter where you come down on the issue of aggressive/violent video games, have a standard and stick with it. Even if your teen doesn't agree with your decisions and sees them as restrictive, in the end he will have a greater respect for you when you stick by what you say.

My sixteen year old is just like every other boy that likes playing video games. He would play as long as he could and anything he could were there no boundaries set on him. No matter how many times I say "no" to more "M" rated games, he keeps asking. He doesn't see the big deal with playing games that I think are out of bounds. Does this sound like your own son?

TWEET IT

Worried about the video games your son is playing? Check out this video resource that could help.
http://bit.ly/1dyblMf
#techsavvyparent

The reality is I don't expect him to agree or to understand. God made life to be an adventure. We are meant to be risk-takers. We were created to explore and have an eye for wonder. Not to mention, what boy doesn't like the opportunity to blow something up every once in a while?

Part of adolescence is experiencing risk. For most boys, the only sense of risk in their lives is living vicariously through their characters in a video game. I don't fault the boys for pushing the boundaries of what is acceptible in games. If my son didn't push the boundaries, I would think something is wrong. Even with this reality, it doesn't excuse the excessive violence and sexism in many of the popular games. The constant tension we face as parents is to provide a real world experience that is even more engaging and exciting than what any video game could offer.

Understanding Video Game Ratings

You walk into your local department store with your child's birthday list in hand. However, it's a list of nothing but video games. There is a traditional board game tacked on the end of the list, but you're convinced it was only added to make you happy.

As you make your way to the back of the store, you're met with row after row of video games. Some of the games on the list are immediately cast off by you because of the picture of a decapitated zombie or the scantily-clad racing chick. There are others you're just not sure about. A few look okay but have a big bold "M" on the front, and another looks a little questionable with a big bold "T" on its cover. An already daunting task has just gotten even more intimidating. Don't give up. There is a rhyme and reason for those nifty letters on the front of the games. But to understand them will require a short history lesson.

In the early 90s, the video game industry was going through a revolution in graphics and speed. Game content such as blood, shooting, and slashing moved from being pixilated to more detailed. They were now lifelike. With the ability to make the action as close to the real world as possible, gamemakers started cranking out increasingly violent content. Parenting groups began to protest the gaming companies, and those protests started making traction with politicians.

After Senate hearings in late 1993, the video game industry was given one year to create a plan to self-regulate their video games. Several attempts later, the industry launched the Entertainment Software Ratings Board. The ESRB is made up of non-industry participants such as parents, former principles, teachers, etc. They independently play each game submitted for rating, then give their recommendation based on the content of the game. Although participation in the rating system is purely voluntary, the major gaming-console manufacturers have chosen not to license games that do not have a rating. To date, the ESRB has rated more than 19,000 games. Each of the rating categories are listed along with a brief description.

ESRB Content Descriptors

EARLY CHILDHOOD
Titles rated EC (Early Childhood) have content that may be suitable for ages 3 and older. Contains no material that parents would find inappropriate.

EVERYONE
Titles rated E (Everyone) have content that may be suitable for ages 3 and older. Contains no material that parents would find inappropriate.

EVERYONE 10+
Titles rated E10+ (Everyone 10 and older) have content that may be suitable for ages 10 and older. Titles in this category may contain more cartoon, fantasy or mild violence, mild language and/or minimal suggestive themes.

TEEN
Titles rated T (Teen) have content that may be suitable for ages 13 and older. Titles in this category may contain violence, suggestive themes, crude humor, minimal blood, simulated gambling, and/or infrequent use of strong language.

Who's Playing all Those Video Games

3 billion hours of games are played

EACH & EVERY WEEK
AROUND THE WORLD

From the time a boy is born until he turns 18 he will play

100,000 HOURS of Video Games

That is as much time as he would spend in middle and high school with perfect attendance.

Video Game Sales by Rating

45%

EVERYONE

22%

EVERYONE +10

24%

TEEN

9%

MATURE

Mature rated games are the lowest produced, yet they are some of the highest selling franchises

HAL◌

CALL of DUTY

grand theft auto

REVENUE   UNITS

	HALO	CALL OF DUTY	GRAND THEFT AUTO
UNITS	57 million	139 million	143 million
REVENUE	$3.2 billion	$9.3 billion	$9.6 billion

Resource: ESRB, Ratings Report, 2012; Essential Facts About the Computer and Video Game Industry 2013 Sales Demographic and Usage Data, ESA

MATURE

Titles rated M (Mature) have content that may be suitable for persons ages 17 and older. Titles in this category may contain intense violence, blood and gore, sexual content and/or strong language.

ESRB Content Descriptors

That explains the rating symbols on the front of the game packaging, but if you flip to the backside of the case you'll see what are called "content descriptors." These descriptors give the specific reasons for the rating given to the game by the ESRB.

Below are the categories and their explanations. Most of these are self-explanatory. Don't worry, you're not going to be quizzed on these later. I know the list is long, but reading through it once will at least put the knowledge where it needs to be so you can recall it later when you're standing in the aisle at Best Buy.

- **Alcohol Reference** - Reference to and/or images of alcoholic beverages
- **Animated Blood** - Discolored and/or unrealistic depictions of blood
- **Blood** - Depictions of blood
- **Blood and Gore** - Depictions of blood or the mutilation of body parts
- **Cartoon Violence** - Violent actions involving cartoon-like situations and characters; may include violence where a character is unharmed after the action has been inflicted
- **Comic Mischief** - Depictions or dialogue involving slapstick or suggestive humor
- **Crude Humor** - Depictions or dialogue involving vulgar antics, including "bathroom" humor

- **Drug Reference** - Reference to and/or images of illegal drugs
- **Fantasy Violence** - Violent actions of a fantasy nature, involving human or non-human characters in situations easily distinguishable from real life
- **Intense Violence** - Graphic and realistic-looking depictions of physical conflict; may involve extreme and/or realistic blood, gore, weapons, and depictions of human injury and death
- **Language** - Mild to moderate use of profanity
- **Lyrics** - Mild references to profanity, sexuality, violence, alcohol or drug use in music
- **Mature Humor** - Depictions or dialogue involving "adult" humor, including sexual references
- **Nudity** - Graphic or prolonged depictions of nudity
- **Partial Nudity** - Brief and/or mild depictions of nudity
- **Real Gambling** - Player can gamble, including betting or wagering real cash or currency
- **Sexual Content** - Non-explicit depictions of sexual behavior, possibly including partial nudity
- **Sexual Themes** - References to sex or sexuality

- **Sexual Violence** - Depictions of rape or other violent sexual acts
- **Simulated Gambling** - Player can gamble without betting or wagering real cash or currency
- **Strong Language** - Explicit and/or frequent use of profanity
- **Strong Lyrics** - Explicit and/or frequent references to profanity, sex, violence, alcohol or drug use in music
- **Strong Sexual Content** - Explicit and/or frequent depictions of sexual behavior, possibly including nudity
- **Suggestive Themes** - Mild provocative references or materials
- **Use of Drugs** - The consumption or use of illegal drugs
- **Use of Alcohol** - The consumption of alcoholic beverages
- **Use of Tobacco** - The consumption of tobacco products
- **Violence** - Scenes involving aggressive conflict; may contain bloodless dismemberment

All of this can be a lot to remember, especially when you're standing in the aisle of a big box store surrounded by hundreds of games. To make it a little easier on you as a parent, the ESRB has created a mobile app for iPhone, Android, and Windows phones. If you have a smartphone, simply search the app store and download to your phone. The next time you're standing in a store looking at a game, open the app. Type in the name of the game you want details on, or snap a picture of the cover and the app will find the game info for you.

With the app on your phone and this knowledge in your head, you are now several steps ahead of most parents in understanding what kids are playing. And you can feel more confident in giving an informed "yes" or "no" to your child's next request for the latest game.

Social Networking Etiquette for Parents: Facebook & Instagram Faux Pas

"Don't you wish there was a repellent you could spray on your parents whenever they embarrass you in public?"
—Teen on Facebook

One of the greatest fears for a teenager is that they would be embarrassed by a parent in public. I remember not wanting to walk with my mom through the mall for fear that one of my friends would walk up and hear words tumble out of my mom's mouth that would make my eyes roll back in my

Parents Get on Social Media Train

As early adopters of new technologies, teenagers are able to help launch new social media sites with great fanfare. Parents take **2 YEARS** to catch up. Here is how the top five social engines fare in parent participation.

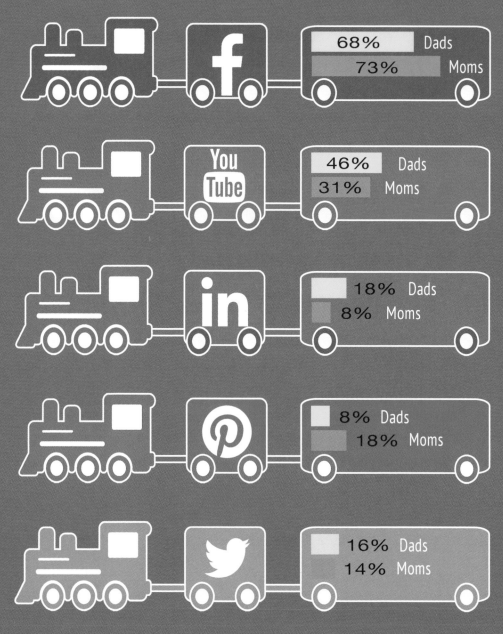

	Dads	Moms
facebook	68%	73%
YouTube	46%	31%
in	18%	8%
Pinterest	8%	18%
Twitter	16%	14%

Source: "State of the American Mom 2012," Marketing to Moms Coalition, 2012.

head. With Facebook's 1.2 billion members and Instagram's 200 million members, these have become the shopping mall of the new millennium. This also means that they are the new places where the typical teen breaks out in beads of sweat when they see that a parent has joined.

There is nothing wrong with parents being on Facebook, Instagram, Twitter, or any other "all the rage" social app that comes out. I think we should be there. It's a public forum and a great way to keep up with what is happening in society. There's also nothing wrong with parents liking, tweeting, or being "friends" with their teen on Facebook. As a matter of personal opinion, I think you absolutely should. I don't understand "parenting experts" who say you should respect your teen's privacy by not "friending" them online. If you have a good relationship with your teen offline, then it is certainly possible to have a good one online. But the key to having a success-ful relationship with your teen on a social network such as Facebook is yours to win or lose based on your ability to avoid the social faux pas land mines.

Many a parent has stumbled onto one of these land mines completely unintentionally. I don't know many parents that willfully set out to embarrass their teenagers. It's usually an "oops" moment that seems harmless enough to you, but makes your child's eyes bug out muttering under his breath, "What were you think-ing?" Here are five key destructive actions to stay away from.

1. **Beware of Posting Potentially Embarrassing Photos of Them.** More than half of all parents on Instagram, Pinterest, and Facebook post pictures of their children at least three times each week. Far too often they post pictures they think are "oh, so cute" of their son's first bath or daughter dressed like an Oompaloompa from her third grade play. But believe me, these will be met with a shrieking, "Noooo!" when your teen sees them online plastered for the whole world to see. The picture of your whole family dressed in white polos at the beach is passable without getting permission, but for all others, I would recommend asking your child before posting. Chances are your teen won't mind you sharing with your Facebook buddies the pics of them in the Karate competition or at the ballet recital. But the habit of asking first shows your teenager that you respect how people perceive them in public.

2. **Beware of Posting Embarrassing Photos of Yourself.** After all the time you spent training your teen not to share inappropriate photos of herself online, don't blow it by doing just the opposite yourself. Pictures of you and your coworkers toasting at the office Christmas party with your Heinekens held high may be a good memory, but it's definitely not one for everyone to see. Likewise, the muscle-flexing shot of you on the beach last summer is out of the question. You might think it's cool or funny, but your teen is going to flee. Remember your teen can see everything you post.

3. **Keep Comments to a Minimum.** Occasional comments on your teen's profile is fine, but keep them short and sweet. And don't comment on everything they post. You wouldn't do that to another friend on social media site so don't do it to your teenager either. I would also recommend testing the waters first. Start off with simple responses every once in a while and go from there as you build trust and she sees you're not taking advantage of being able to see everything she posts.

4. No Lecturing Online.
Let's just assume that your daughter is going to be like most teen girls, and at some point in time she is going to post or say something online that she shouldn't. It could be that she is not the one who posts something inappropriate, but rather one of her friends posts something to her page. Don't confront her online, unless your goal is to isolate and ridicule. Instead, talk about it in person. Be honest with her about how you feel about what her friend posted on your daughter's page. Remind her of the boundaries you both discussed before you allowed her to be on Facebook or Instagram. Then ask her to remove it. Make the conversation brief, but if the behavior continues you need to have a "sit down."

5. Keep the Friend Circle Tight.
Part of a teenager's self-identity is wrapped up in who they know and how many people they know in their ever-increasing circle of friends. When you look at your teen's profile and it shows she has 942 friends and you only have 113, don't let that bother you. Your goal is not to be friends with every one of your teen's friends. You don't hang out in your daughter's bedroom when her friends are over because that would be a little weird. It's the same way online. She needs space to interact with her friends without you being part of every conversation.

On the same note, please, please don't send friend requests to her friends. It can look creepy and inappropriate. If one of the girls from her soccer team or church youth group sends you a friend request, you should tell your teen before accepting. It keeps everything out in the open. Otherwise, she will feel like you are encroaching on her territory.

The Healthy Disconnect

I'm sure you've had the experience of being a carpool mom (or dad). You've got your middle schooler and five of her friends crammed in the minivan. On the way to drop them off at the school football game, they start chattering. They talk, and talk, and talk. As you are driving, you are also listening and learning. While sitting in the backseats, the girls start spilling to one another about what boys they are crushing on that week, who did something embarrassing at school, and which teachers they don't like. Being a smart parent, you don't comment. You're like a cultural anthropologist being given rare insight into a different culture.

Being your teenager's friend online is much like your carpool experience. You are going to learn things about your child that maybe she hasn't shared with you yet. As long as she is exhibiting good choices online, there is no need for you to respond to everything you see and hear. She needs the space from you, within reason, to create a canvass of herself online. Let her be herself and consider it a privilege that you get to be a part of the experience.

It is possible to have a good online relationship with your teen, just like you enjoy offline. But a good relationship will require you to play an even greater balancing act of being a watchful and trusting parent. If you've built a relationship of trust, taught appropriate social behavior, and treated your teen with respect, then this can continue as she ventures online.

How Young Is Too Young for Facebook?

(and other social media)

Our son turned thirteen. Successfully reaching the milestone, we officially said "goodbye" to childhood and dove into the teenage years. It's also the day our son wanted an answer to his year-long question, "Can I have a Facebook account?" It's a question thousands of parents have to answer every day.

Up until now, it's been an easy question to answer. Facebook's registration requirement states that a person must be at least thirteen years old in order to have an account. Appar-

ently, Facebook is getting more serious about keeping kids safe online by keeping them off of their site. I recently read that Facebook removes 20,000 under-age-thirteen profiles from their site each day. But, in the long run, is it that big of a deal?

It would be easy to say, "Who really cares if I let my eleven year old on Facebook? Who would ever know anyway?" There are several reasons why it matters, and they all come back to character. For one, I would know… and my son would know. I've been teaching him that integrity is what you do even when no one is watching. Character is created by the small decisions we make. So, to tell a small lie when no one will know and no one will get hurt, yeah, it still matters.

Mark Twain called honesty a "lost art" while William Shakespeare dubbed it, "the best policy." Being honest with others is an extension of being honest with myself. Integrity flows out of our core and largely determines the health of our relationships with our family. The Apostle Paul even pointed to the direct source for his character in writing, "Follow my example, as I follow the example of Christ." If honesty and integrity are the character qualities you want developed in your children, then that is the kind of character you must model. And it includes being truthful even in the small things such as whether or not you will lie so your preteen can get on Facebook.

Unintended Consequences of COPPA

The other problem is that everything a teen shares online is culled by Facebook (or Google, YouTube, etc.) to form a consumer profile of each user. Facebook then uses that information to generate ads, suggest groups, or most notoriously, they will sell your teen's information to advertisers and marketing groups. In short, **everything your student says, good or bad, can be used for someone else to make money.**

In 1998, Congress created the Children's Online Privacy Protection Act (COPPA). It requires the Federal Trade Commission to regulate Website operators whose sites are created for children or that children are likely to visit. COPPA prohibits websites from soliciting information from children under the age of 13 without their parents' knowledge.

The intent of Congress was to protect children from predatory or manipulative marketing and safety risks such as online stalking that could very easily turn into real-world stalking. It's a good piece of legislation that we should all support. The only way the law doesn't get enforced is when children lie about their age to get onto a website, or worse, when their parent lies for them. Waiting to let your child be on Facebook is not only good for their safety, it also lets you model integrity in small decisions. And it's the law.

I'm certain you would agree that your child's safety is important to you, and that you want to model a proper character to your child. Yet it's remarkable just how many under-age-13 children are on Facebook. According to a study by First Monday, more than half of all kids join Facebook before age thirteen. To break it down, 32% of eleven year olds and 55% of all twelve year olds are already on

underage on facebook

	current age of child			
	10	**11**	**12**	**13**
Mean age child joined Facebook	8.9	10.0	11.1	12.1
Parent was aware child joined	95%	88%	82%	82%
Parent helped create account	78%	68%	76%	60%

Go right ahead!

Parents who thought it better to **LIE** rather than make their children wait.

% of all underage children with a facebook profile

19% — 10 yr olds
32% — 11 yr olds
55% — 12 yr olds
69% — 13 yr olds

That is more than **7.5M** underage children in America on facebook.

88% of these parents said it was okay if their child lied to be on facebook.

Only **53%** of parents are aware that facebook has a minimum age requirement.

Source:"Why Parents Lie to Let Their Kids on Facebook" First Monday, Vol. 16, Num. 11, 2011

Facebook. Basically, half of all eleven and twelve year olds have lied to get onto a website. Even more startling is the number of parents who not only knew about their kids' actions, but helped carry out the lie.

It is peculiar what happens with parental involvement though. If the child is under age thirteen, it's more likely the parent is aware of the child being on Facebook and more likely to wrongly help setup the account. But once the child is over thirteen, it's as if the parent drops out of the picture. Instead of leaving your thirteen year old to his own devices on Facebook, you should use the opportunity to help him use the website in an appropriate and safe manner.

Facebook Safety Center

One of the easiest ways to help your anxious teenager start his Facebook experience off on the right foot is by utilizing the Facebook Safety Center. Not only will it be a good educational tool for your teen, but it will help take some of the guesswork out of the equation for you. Instead of you trying to remember all the right things to talk about, Facebook has attempted to organize it for you.

The Family Safety Center is divided into four separate sections: Parents, Teens, Teachers and Law Enforcement. Each section addresses questions specific to that audience. I appreciate Facebook's forward thinking to equip law enforcement officers with tools to prevent cyberstalking and tips for tracking sex crime offenders who

Teachers
Learn and teach about how to use social media wisely.

Parents
Help your teens play it safe on Facebook.

Teens
Be smart. Use good judgment whenever you're online.

Law Enforcement
Learn how Facebook works with your local law enforcement.

have registered with the site. Teachers are given tips for using social media in the classroom and where to report inappropriate use of the site.

The Parent Section will help you to understand the basic layout of Facebook, how to set safe boundaries online, and how to address issues such as online etiquette with your teen. The Teen Section walks teens through how to set privacy settings on their profile, who to talk to if they are being contacted by a stranger, and the importance of thinking before posting. Reading through the short articles will make you aware of the issues at stake (including the ones you don't know about yet) and prepare you to bring these up with your Facebook rookie. There are even articles to help you if, God forbid, your teen does become a victim of cyberbullying or a similar offense.

This is not meant as an endorsement for Facebook. But they are making it easier to start a dialogue with your young teen. IF they will be on the site, they can do so in a safe way. You can even do what our family did. Before agreeing to let your thirteen year old have a Facebook profile, make him read the information in the Safety Center then give him a quiz. If he passes, then he's one step closer to earning the privilege (and your trust) of being on Facebook. I'm not sure my son enjoyed my turning Facebook safety into a school-type assignment with a grade, but it did raise the bar for him in terms of our expectations and created a higher level of responsibility. In the end, he saw that being on Facebook was a privilege and not just another thing we quickly say "yes" to without jumping through a few appropriate hoops.

Facebook Preparedness Checklist

The following is a list of issues to discuss with your young teen before letting them set up a profile on Facebook. You may even want to type these up to create your own Facebook Contract. Have your teen initial each one along with any other issues you come up with.

Both of you can sign it as a way of agreeing on what is and is not allowed with this new medium.

1. **Profile to Private:** Your profile should ALWAYS be set to "private." This allows only people that are your "friends" to see your profile, postings, photos, etc.

2. **Prudence in Posting:** Anything your friends see on your profile can be passed on to anyone else, so be mindful of what you say and how you say it on your private profile. In 2013 Facebook changed their posting abilities for teens. You can now share your posts with the whole world instead of just your friends. Be sure to always answer to "Friends only" when asked who you would like to see your posts.

3. **Permanence of Posts:** When you post something on Facebook, it is retrievable forever by Facebook. They are allowed to use anything you say in promoting or advertising their products. Basically, your posts belong to them.

4. **Pictures Speak Louder than Words:** Any picture you post can be saved by someone else and passed on to anyone they want. Before posting a photo, ask yourself, "Do I really want anyone seeing me in that bathing suit, at that party, holding that sign, etc.?"

Never post a child's photo without their parent's consent, even if it is a friend of yours.

5. **Bullying is Never Cool:** Words hurt, especially when they tear down someone's character or value. Never post something that is demeaning to someone else even if you only mean it as a joke. Think of bullying like a snowball tumbling down a hill. Once it starts, it is difficult to stop and only gets bigger as time goes on.

6. **Moderation is the Key:** Even though finding community and friendships on Facebook is a normal activity of our generation, it can never take the place of face-to-face time with friends and family. Set limits for yourself concerning how much time you'll be on Facebook each day.

Shifting Sands of Social Media

Recently, Facebook has been taking some licks from teenagers. The problem is not so much Facebook's fault as it is parents'. As more and more parents (and grandparents) have joined facebook, teenagers feel they have no privacy on the site. They feel they can no longer be fully transparent without a parent looking over their shoulder.

This has become a double-edged sword for parents. **I believe that if your teenager is going to be on Facebook, then you should be on Facebook.** But the more time you spend on the site, the more likely your teen is to flee the site. Growth in other sites such as Tumblr and Instagram and apps like Snapshat, ask.fm, and kik, can be directly linked to teen flight from Facebook. However, more than 3 in 4 of all teens still check their Facebook profile at least once a day so it's not like the sky is falling for Facebook yet. If you want to know where your teenager is online, it's still the first place to check.

Your Teen's Social Media Fingerprint

It is important to understand potential dangers of your teen's social media usage and the fingerprint they leave behind on each site.

The *ask.fm* app used for Q&A is rife with verbal abuse and cyberbullying.

Tumblr has no age or content restrictions. It's the wild west of blogging sites.

Snapchat is hugely popular with teens. Known for sexting & other inappropriate content.

Besides Facebook, *Instagram* is the most popular site for teens. There are no age or content restrictions, but your posts can be set to private so only friends can see.

Teenagers are what are called "first adoptors" of social media. They will always be the first one to try a new site or app. If a site becomes a hit in pop culture, it is typically because of its understanding of the teenage world and it's ability to let teenagers share as openly as possible. New social media sites directed toward a teen/young single audience are launched literally every month. Most of them fall flat, but a few stick and take off like a virus.

Facebook may have an age restriction of thirteen, but you can't assume it is the same for all sites. The age restrictions come back to the COPPA law we discussed earlier. If the site is going to collect your browsing information and use it to market something to you, then the minimum age allowed by law is thirteen. **Facebook makes its money through targeted ads to users**, but this is another factor that turns teenagers off. They don't like how commercial Facebook is becoming.

New social networking sites such as Tumblr and Instagram have decided against direct marketing so they don't have to have an age restriction. This means any age is welcome. Your eight, nine, or ten year old can have an account...and they do! Well, maybe not your child, but there are plenty of others on there.

The same principles you teach your tween to follow in what is appropriate and out of bounds for Facebook has to be talked about again and again for all the other sites (or apps) they want to be on. It is okay to say "yes" to some and "no" to others, but be sure to give your teen or tween a clear answer as to why you do not approve of a particular site. Join all of the sites yourself, not to snoop, but to give good accountability. Periodically check her activity on the sites. Part of your ongoing conversation about social media needs to be about what what's new out there and what is she looking at now.

Benefits of Delaying the Inevitable

Admittedly, I've been a rebel my whole life. I question everything and always want to know the "why" behind any rule. I want my children to have a little of that independence and willingness to ask questions, but I also want them to see authority differently than I did. We want to teach our teenagers how to live under proper authority and that reasonable rules are a healthy part of life. Facebook has not said, "You can't ever be on our site," nor have we said that to our children. We've simply said, "Not yet." Sometimes delayed gratification can be even more satisfying than immediate pleasure. In a culture where almost everything is instantaneous, won't it be worth it to wait just a few more precious months for Facebook?

Saying "No, not yet" has given us a period of time to model for our son (and for our daughter, who prefers Instagram) how to use social media properly. We've had conversations about what not to post online, the permanence of posts, being mindful of your comments to others online, and how quickly posts and photos can be picked up and reposted by others. Now they seem prepared for the plunge, instead of being thrown in the deep waters and figuring it out along the way. My teens (and yours) are going to make mistakes online, but by taking the time to create a healthy foundation *now* they will have a better chance of finding a healthy balance.

Importance of
Facebook Privacy
Controls

If you are a mom, you can probably remember getting your first diary as a little girl. You would spend time alone in your bedroom scribbling down your most private thoughts. What you did with your friends, who the cute boy at school was that particular week, and what you thought of your parents were common themes. You would have been mortified if anyone ever read your most personal thoughts and saw that picture of your "crush" hidden in the pages.

So what did you do with all those juicy thoughts once you wrote them down? You locked your diary and told no one where you hid the key. Can you imagine someone taking all of your private thoughts, memories, and daily activities and posting them online for the whole world (literally) to see. This is exactly what has happened with Facebook, YouTube, Pinterest, and other social networking sites.

While in a youth pastor's office one day we were looking at Facebook profiles of middle schoolers in his ministry. We were particularly interested to see what kinds of things students in this age group were talking about online. There were the usual silly photos, links to favorite videos, and talk of the previous day's activities, but one particular student's profile caught our attention.

This innocent looking seventh grader was using the notes app to keep her online diary. Only this diary wasn't under lock and key—it was there for anyone and everyone to read. She didn't post anything scandalous or sexual. As a matter of fact, most of it was about noth-

Dear Diary, what should I share today?

Girls use diaries more than ever before, but sometimes without discretion of where they write.

83% of 16-19 year old girls keep a pen-and-paper diary.

95% of teen girls say that they keep their deepest secrets off of Facebook.

78% say that they are worried about posting their feelings on social media.

Despite this 71% still post personal information on Facebook and Twitter.

Source: Market study for E4 launch of My Big Fat Diary, Otherlines.tv, 2013.

ing in particular. But in her ramblings of everyday middle school life, she told us everything we didn't need to know. She listed her middle school, her class schedule, a picture of her house with her address, her favorite activities, and her cell phone number. Yes, her cell number. She even mentioned that she took French horn lessons on Thursday afternoons at 4PM at her church.

It wasn't like this girl was an idiot. She didn't list all of this information in a bullet form list. Instead, over the course of several weeks of posting about her normal daily life, she mentioned bits of personal information here and there. But over the course of time, she shared enough that if someone was of evil intent, they would have everything they need to establish a relationship with this girl.

Stopping It Before It Ever Starts

If you are ready for your 13 year old to take the inevitable plunge onto Facebook, it is imperative that he understand the importance of Facebook Privacy Controls outlined in the previous chapter. He also needs to hear from you that setting privacy controls has nothing to do with you trying to control him, but rather it is to protect him. You can assure him that he won't be the weirdo in his group. Chances are most teens older than him have already learned the hard lesson that comes from letting just anyone see their profiles.

When Facebook was first started, less than ten percent of teens had their profile set to private, but today more than 70% of them have enabled this function. **Setting your profile to private is the initial step in protecting your online identity.** This keeps anyone who is not a "friend" from seeing your profile and let's you control the flow of information. However, keep in mind that Facebook always has access to anything you post.

In those early days of Facebook, and MySpace before it, cyberbullying was rampant with aggressive users harassing other teens by posting a message on another person's profile. There have also been a number of cases of stalking by adults that would try and form a relationship with a minor. National news stories have featured teens humiliated because of things they said or photos they posted that *they thought only their friends could see*. Instead, they shared their most private thoughts with their whole school.

None of this is meant to scare you, but rather to show what is possible. It is possible for Facebook and other sites to be enjoyable if you help teach your teen to take measures to protect themselves. By taking advantage of the privacy features built in Facebook, you can stop any of the mentioned scenarios before it ever starts.

Finding the Privacy Settings

Facebook has tried to make setting the privacy controls as simple as possible, but there is still much to wade through. But don't worry, I'm going to show you the most important parts and how to find them.

To access the privacy controls, click on the small white lock next to the gear-shaped button. Then click on "privacy controls." Yes, I know that was obvious, but the rest might not be.

The first thing you want to help your teen do is determine their Default Privacy Setting for posting. This specifically refers to posts made using third party apps such as a Facebook app for iPhone, iPod, or Android phones. These apps don't let you select your privacy setting for each individual post, so the app looks to what you have set as your default setting on the Facebook site.

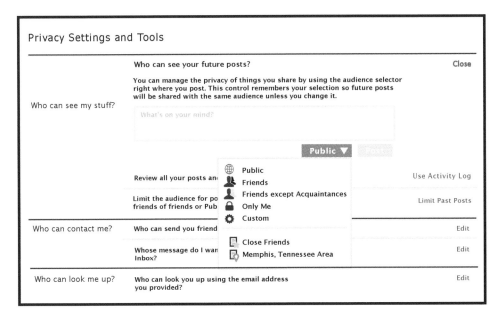

The default setting Facebook assigns is Public. This means that anyone else on Facebook is able to see what your teen has posted. A safer alternative is to select **Friends.** This option confines the viewers to only those people that are on your teen's friend list. The last option is "Custom." With this option you can make it even more specific who can and cannot see your teen's postings. When you se-lect "Custom," it will bring up a pop up window that let's you select your restrictions.

From the drop down menu, if you select **Specific People or Lists**, you can type in a smaller group of people that can see the postings. A list is a group that you create in the friends section. For instance, you can create a list called "Family" or "BFFs." When you come back to this Custom Privacy Screen, you simply type in your list name. Now only those few people can see the postings.

Another option here is the Don't Share This With function. This allows you to hide specific people or lists from being able to see your teen's postings. Basically, it's the reverse way of blocking viewers. Insist that your teen not block you from seeing their posts.

Custom Privacy

✓ **Share this with** ──────────────────────────

These people or lists: [Specific People or Lists... ⬍]

[   ]

Note: Anyone tagged can also see this
post.

✗ **Don't share this with** ──────────────────

These people or lists: [   ]

[**Save Changes**] [Cancel]

After determining your Default Privacy Controls, it's time to dial
into some more specific areas of restrictions. You'll find these just
below the Default Privacy Controls.

There's a lot to look at here so don't get too overwhelmed. Take it
slow and spend some time reading over all the options before making any changes. It's not imperative to restrict everything now, but
there are a few categories with options that should be turned off for
a Facebook newbie. We're going to look at the three most important.

First click on "Edit Settings" on the How You Connect option.

There are two options to restrict here. Under "Who can look you
up" turn the option to **Friends of Friends** only. When you reg-
ister with Facebook you have to provide a cell phone number and
email address. In case a stranger comes across your provided cell
number or email on the internet, you don't want them typing it into
a Facebook search and finding your teen's profile. The second thing

to do is click on the "Who can send you Facebook messages."
Definitely turn this option to **Friends Only.** If this is set to "Everyone," then anyone else on Facebook, including that creepy fifty year
old that still listens to Wham!, can send your teenage messages. Setting the option to Friends Only will only allow people that your teen
knows to be able to send them messages.

One of the first ways that young teens exhibit poor boundaries on
Facebook is by responding to messages from strangers. I can't state
strongly enough how important it is to talk with your teen about
this and restrict who can send your teen messages. Part of the trust
you are giving your teen in allowing him to be on Facebook is that
you won't know everyone on his friend list. If you are your teen's
friend on Facebook, which you absolutely should be, then you can
see his friend list. But that doesn't mean you'll know all the other
people on there. It can make you feel overwhelmed seeing a list of
so many people on Facebook with whom your teen is connected.

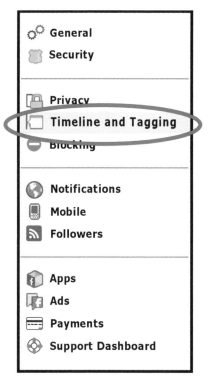

All of those people can send your teen
messages that you will never see, and
this takes a degree of trust on your
part. At the very least, you want to keep
as tight as possible the circle of people
who can send your teenager messages.

The next area of restrictions you need
to look at is under Timeline and
Tagging. In 2012, Facebook intro-
duced a feature called the Timeline.
Basically, your timeline is a visual
picture of your life on Facebook. For
instance, it might list things like when
you joined Facebook, where your
first job was, who you took to prom,
or when you graduated from college.
Think of it as a Wikipedia about your

Timeline and Tagging Settings

Who can add things to my timeline?	Who can post on your timeline?	Friends
	Review posts friends tag you in before they appear on your timeline?	On
Who can see things on my timeline?	Review what other people see on your timeline	
	Who can see posts you've been tagged in on your timeline?	**Everyone**
	Who can see what others post on your timeline?	**Everyone**
How can I manage tags people add and tagging suggestions?	Review tags people add to your own posts before the tags appear on Facebook?	On
	When you're tagged in a post, who do you want to add to the audience if they aren't already in it?	**Friends**
	Who sees tag suggestions when photos that look like you are uploaded?	**Friends**

life. Tagging, on the other hand, is sort of like a digital autograph for a Facebook post. Say you take a picture of your family vacation and upload it to your profile. You can "tag" yourself, your spouse, and your teen so the photo is now associated with their profiles as well. Now if someone looks up your teen on Facebook, besides the posts he has made, they will also find the picture you uploaded.

In the Timeline and Tagging section, you want to set "Who can Post on Your Timeline" to Friends only. This will keep anyone who is not their friend from adding something to your teen's timeline. The other restriction to set is "Review posts friends tag you in before they appear on your timeline." This should be set to On. This will allow your teen to approve or decline any attempt for someone to tag them in a post. It may not be that big of a deal if a friend tags him in a picture of the two of them at a school football game, but if the picture is potentially embarrassing or inappropriate, you want your teenager to be able to say "no thanks" before his reputation is harmed.

The last area you should address is under the Blocked People and Apps section. This section allows you to block individuals, events, or apps. For instance, if a peer was being a cyberbully to your teen and posting inappropriate comments on his profile, he can block just that one peer. Just make sure that your teen doesn't put you on their blocked list, but that is a conversation for another chapter.

Blocking apps is important for any Facebook user, but particularly so for a younger teen. As with smartphones, there are apps for everything you can imagine on Facebook. Besides being an incredible waste of time, the real danger of apps is you have to grant the creator of the app access to your profile contents in order to use their app. You also give the creator of the app permission to post to your page. For instance, if your son thinks Farmville sounds fun and clicks "yes" to using the app, Zynga (the creators) now has his email address, cell number, interest list, bio, etc. Even if he later blocks Farmville, Zynga does not have to delete his info from their system.

Some apps that sound fun could later hurt his reputation or cause

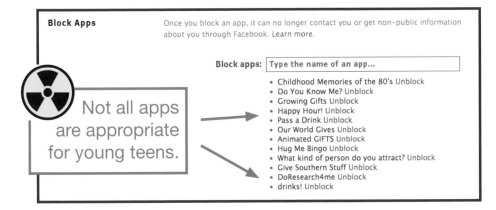

Not all apps are appropriate for young teens.

someone to question his character. Remember the creator of the app has been given permission by your teen to post things such as game results, usage, top score, etc. to his profile. "Ben just planted an acre of corn on Farmville," may sound innocent, but "Ben hit the jackpot in Saloon Slots" or "Ben made a margarita on Pass Me a Drink" doesn't have quite the same ring to it. Unfortunately, there is no way to block all apps. The best you can do is talk to your teen about the long-term benefits of saying no to the app craziness.

Check and Recheck

One other word of caution, as if all of this hasn't scared you away enough, Facebook continually changes the functions and process of their privacy settings. There have been outcries from Facebook users the world over because of the company randomly changing the privacy settings without making it clear to the users.

When the Timeline feature appeared without notice on users' profiles, everything was categorized as public. Let's say you had previously posted a video of yourself dressed as Santa Claus dancing on your kitchen table. There you are in all your red and white glory. It is admittedly funny, but you didn't want the whole world to see, so you labeled the video as viewable to **Friends Only.** Facebook put the video in your Timeline as public for everyone to watch. This became an immediate embarrassment for tens of thousands of users, when parts of their lives were exposed that they intentionally wanted to remain private.

Just because you've taken the time to help your teen set up his Facebook page today doesn't mean it's over. You need to periodically revisit the Privacy Settings to make sure everything is still as it needs to be. Start by looking at the settings on your own page. I know there is a lot to wade through, especially if you are new to Facebook yourself, but it will be worth it for your peace of mind and your teen's safety.

HELPING YOUR TEENS PROTECT THEIR ONLINE REPUTATION

Imagine that from the time of his childhood, it has been your son's dream to play professional baseball. He is in awe of the home-run hitting power of his hero Albert Pujols and the fastball of phenom Stephen Strasburg. He has posters in his room of his favorite players and his shelves lined with bobblehead dolls of players and countless Little League trophies. Baseball is his life.

When high school rolls around, he is on track to get an athletic scholarship that will get him to the next level. From working out and eating healthy to attending training camps and watching game film, he has a game plan to get him where he wants to be. During his senior year, the scouts from colleges are showing up. Everything is going just as he planned to get into his favored school with a rich baseball heritage.

In the spring, scholarship offers come in one after another, but none of them matter compared to the one he received from his dream school. After accepting the offer, the school's athletic department begins taking a serious look into the character behind the athlete that is your son. They want him to come play ball, but they have a couple of red flags to bring to his attention.

He gets an email from the athletic office cautioning him about some sexist rap lyrics he posted on his Facebook profile. They ask him to remove them. A week later comes a phone call telling him that he needs to consider canceling his Twitter account. There are concerns about the racy comments he made about women in a couple recent tweets and the ongoing Twitter conversation it started. Later he receives a call from one of his future teammates telling your son that the picture that just appeared on your son's best friend's profile of them at a keg party is a serious violation of the team's code of conduct and he needs to make sure it gets taken down right away.

A mere two months after getting the scholarship offer letter from the school, another letter arrives. Only this letter states that due to recent events, the school has reconsidered their offer of scholarship and wishes him the best of luck with his future. All the years of work, all the years of doing it the right way are gone because of a few online mistakes. They might seem small in the big scheme of things. Some were not even his fault. But to the college it was too much of a risk. And just like that, it's all over.

Don't think this is a scare tactic or even a rare story. All you need to do is a Google search for "student loses scholarship over Facebook," and the results are endless. From baseball and basketball scholarships to full-ride academic offers, schools are reconsidering financial rewards because of students' online reputations.

What Colleges are Looking for

It used to be that when a high school senior was applying for college, all a school cared about was the right GPA and scores on the ACT or SAT. Since revenue has shrunk at most schools, they have gotten more selective about who they give scholarship dollars to. In the digital age with online profiles, the prospect of getting money from schools has become more and more rigorous. I don't fault the school. It's their money after all, and they can give or withhold to whomever they wish.

Social networking has given schools a bird's-eye view into the life of a prospective student. For better or worse, what they see on a student's profile gives them a caricature of who that student is. Most of the time it's not a complete or accurate picture of the teenager, and it's probably not fair, but it's all they have to go on.

Look at the following two students. Assume that both students have a 3.91 GPA, made a 30 on the ACT, are members of the National Honor Society, and lettered in a sport. Each one also has a Facebook,

* Member of "Teen Voter Rights" Group Page.
* Fan of Humane Society page.
* Posted pictures from Habitat for Humanity work project.
* Posted pics of family vacation.
* Posted comments about friend's mission trip to Equador.

+ Favorite music is Insane Clown Posse
+ Likes DeathMetalRap Fan Page.
+ Member of TN Militia Group Page.
+ Fan of "Legalize Pot Now!" Page.
+ Posted comments on "Hometown Hotties" Group Page.
+ Posted pictures of wild keg party.

Twitter, and Instagram profile that reveals much about interests and activities.

The information doesn't tell you their aspirations for the future, their habits, or what drives them. But it does anecdotally give you insight into their worldview, and colleges will use all this information to create a picture of your teen. Think about it from a school's perspective. If all you had to go on was these few blips of information on a student from Facebook, which one would you want at your school?

Taking the Reins of Your Digital Resume

Seeing the guy's profile, it may be easy to dismiss it as an over-the-top caricature. Maybe your teen's profile looks nothing like this, but what if there was something on there that might be a red flag to a school? Wouldn't it be worth it to delete it now? **Most things done online are merely in good fun or silliness, but when read by just the right person could reflect just the wrong message.** Here are a few tips your college-bound graduate can take to protect his online reputation and communicate an accurate picture of himself.

1. **Restrict Passwords:** Research from the Pew Internet & American Life Project found that 30% of teens who spend regular time online have shared a password with someone; most with a boyfriend or girlfriend. Girls were almost twice as likely to share a password. This can only end badly when the couple breaks up. In adolescence, relationships fizzle out more quickly than boy bands. Passwords should never be shared. For good measure consider telling your teen to change his password at the start of each school year and to keep a master list of all his passwords in a safe place offline.

2. **Setup Notifications:** All social networking sites allow for notification if someone posts someone about you and tags you in a picture. For example, if you set up notifications in Facebook, the site will notify you whenever your name is mentioned anywhere on the site. This is important so that your teen can delete anything that may be inappropriate or potentially embarrassing such as that group photo at last year's New Year's Eve Party with everyone making gang hand signs.

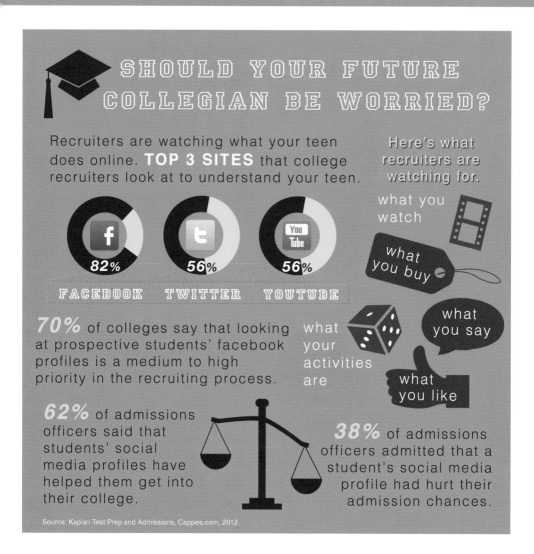

SHOULD YOUR FUTURE COLLEGIAN BE WORRIED?

Recruiters are watching what your teen does online. **TOP 3 SITES** that college recruiters look at to understand your teen.

Here's what recruiters are watching for.

what you watch

what you buy

82% — FACEBOOK

56% — TWITTER

56% — YOUTUBE

70% of colleges say that looking at prospective students' facebook profiles is a medium to high priority in the recruiting process.

what your activities are

what you say

what you like

62% of admissions officers said that students' social media profiles have helped them get into their college.

38% of admissions officers admitted that a student's social media profile had hurt their admission chances.

Source: Kaplan Test Prep and Admissions, Cappes.com, 2012.

3. **Tighten Up Posting:** Facebook (and other social network sites) now have the ability to restrict comments or posts to your profile until you approve of it first. If your teen sets up this function, he would get an email from Facebook notifying him that someone has made a comment and would like permission to allow it. For instance, say your daughter posts photos of herself and some girlfriends from a trip at the beach. The next thing you know guys start posting some not-so-innocent comments about how the girls look in their bathing suits. If comment restriction had been turned on, none of the crude comments would have been posted.

4. **Google Yourself:** No, this isn't a vain attempt to see how popular you are. Doing a Google search of yourself lets you see where your name or likeness appears on other sites. If your name is out there, Google will find it. As a parent, Google all of your children once a year regardless of age just to make sure that all is right. While you're at it, do a search in Yahoo and Bing as well. If you create a Google profile, you can set up notifications there making it even easier.

5. **Create a Social List:** As an adult, it's a safe bet to assume you are on Facebook, but not the newest social network site that popped up last month. Teenagers are typically early adopters of new social websites. Instagram was a huge hit among teens and twenty-somethings before most parents ever caught on to it. Even at its peak, MySpace had relatively few adult users compared to teens. Other newer sites such as MyYearbook don't even allow adult participants. Teens who belong to several sites at once tend to migrate often; however, they don't take the time to cancel their old profiles. Because of this, there can be A LOT OF INFORMATION about your teen floating around out there. Have your child keep a list of all the sites for which he has created a user profile.

5. **Control Your Representation:** The easiest way for your teen to control the representation of himself online is to create a blog. Instead of letting others on Facebook speak for him, he's allowed to speak for himself. You can do this for free through sites like Blogger, or purchase your own personalized web address through GoDaddy. It's inexpensive and can actually be a great tool for him to market himself to colleges. He can talk about his interests, community involvement, passions, and aspirations without the headache of others' comments.

Derailing Their Career Plans

It's not only in preparing for college that your teen's online reputation matters. In many ways an even stiffer consequence may be paid when looking for a job after college. It's easy for collegians to let their guard down when using the internet. They got into the college of their choice, but that's only the beginning. Next comes entering into a career—a career that should be the reward of all their hard work.

I'm sure you can remember your own mindset in college. We all did silly and impulsive things—from playing dorm pranks to dressing up for theme parties. But for college students today, all of those memories tend to end up on Facebook, Instagram, or YouTube where the company they want to work for will see all those videos, photographs, and comments. The consequences can end a career before it ever gets started.

CareerBuilder surveyed more than 2,300 hiring managers concerning their hiring practices. **At least 37% use social networking sites to research potential hires.**[1] As you could guess, the reasons for not hiring them all came down to what the applicant unwittingly revealed about themselves online.

53% - *Posted provocative/inappropriate photos or information*

35% - *Posted content about themselves drinking or doing drugs*

29% - *Showed poor communication skills*

26% - *Made discriminatory comments*

On the other hand, there were candidates whose online profiles were an asset to their job application. It was as if their online profile became a confirmation to the hiring manager that the applicant was the same in real life as who they said they were on their application.

50% - *Gave a good representation of themselves*

39% - *Their profile supported their professional qualifications*

38% - *Displayed their creativity*

35% - *Showed good communication skills*

Being the Parent Buffer

As a parent, you see the immediacy with which your teen lives his life. It's hard for him to think four to eight years down the road to how his present on-line actions can effect his future. He's doing good to remember his math homework for tomorrow and to get home before curfew. He's not scrutinizing every impulsive comment he makes on Twitter. That's where you come in.

Teens don't fully grasp the public forum that the internet creates. When we were kids and had a disagreement with a classmate, we would meet on the playground

> ### MODEL IT
> ### FIRST
> When you share a shocking social or political jab online, whether right or not, you are displaying a behavior that could also cost your teen.

after school, push each other around for a few minutes, then go back to being friends tomorrow. Today the shoving match ends up on YouTube after being captured on someone's phone and gets viewed by 167,000 people the first month. When you broke up with someone in middle school, you might have put a note in their locker. Today, it's a post on Facebook followed by an explicative-filled response by the other to your page. And the whole world can see.

Part of your job as a parent is to be a buffer for your teen—to help him see online profiles from an outsider's perspective. Here are a few questions for your college hopeful to ask before posting, friending, liking, or tweeting:

- Would I want my future spouse to see this?
- Would this be embarrassing if my grandmother read this?
- Am I writing this just because I'm angry or hurt?
- Does this clearly communicate who I am?
- Would it be shocking if I saw this on someone else's page?
- Do I want this to always be associated with who I am?
- Does this compromise my faith or personal moral standard?

You've heard the saying, "You only get one chance to make a first impression." Make sure the first impression a future employer sees of your teen is a lasting one, by helping him take control of his own online reputation. Every day your teenager creates a growing organic online resume of his life. Every post, video, and comment becomes a part of his biography. No one else should get to create that resume for him with foolish or misunderstood elements.

Internet Safety is as Important as Locking the Front Door

Can you imagine what it would be like to live in a neighborhood where you never have to lock your doors at night? Or to park your car anywhere you want with no worries of what you leave inside? Let's take it a step farther. Can you imagine not only leaving everything unlocked, but also leaving your keys in the door to make it easier for you to get in the next time?

The scenario sounds so absurd that it's hard not to laugh. It's simply not the world we live in...at least not anymore. If your home was broken into, but you hadn't locked the doors to begin with, the reporting police officer would look at you like you were an idiot. And maybe rightly so.

Don't misunderstand. I'm not talking about living in fear. I'm talking about common sense protection and precautions. Locking the doors both keeps my family safe and keeps me from getting frustrated or angry if something is taken...just in case. That's really what it boils down to, isn't it? Being prepared for the "just in case." We'll go to great lengths to protect our possessions, but when it comes to online safety, many families are incredibly lax. Every day, kids turn on their home computers, pull their tablets out of their backpacks, or carry their cell phones around without any boundaries to protect them from others or from their own poor judgment.

Acting Now is Important

I've lost count of how many emails I've gotten from parents who want to know what to do because they just found out their teenager has been looking at pornography on their computer. No matter how culturally hip a parent tries to be, this is one issue that sends every mother over the edge and rightly so. Online pornography may be the most shocking issue, but it's certainly not the only one. Consider how you would respond to the following scenarios:

- Ð Your son is playing excessively violent multi-player video games with strangers all over the world.

- Ð Your daughter is bombarded with bullying messages from people on Facebook and doesn't know how to make it stop.

- Ð Your tween is talking with strangers on a chat site because "we are all who we say we are."

- Your ten year old comes across one of the more than 20,000 sexually-oriented videos posted to YouTube each day.

- Your daughter is reading pro-Anna (anorexia) websites because of her struggles with her own body image.

- Your son can't set his own time restrictions, can't make himself get offline, and is losing sleep.

If your teen is struggling with any one of these issues, it's not just one area of life that ends up effected. It bleeds over into their social life, their school work, their self-esteem, and their level of trust with you. Wheels can begin to come off in other areas of life because of something you may not even be aware is happening. Instead of reacting when it happens, you can choose to be proactive and set up an internet safety program from the beginning.

My children and I have had countless conversations about purity, pornography, and personal choices. Ultimately, my desire and prayer is that they choose to guard their hearts and minds and make choices that are honoring of themselves, those around them, and the God that made them. This takes a great deal of maturity on their part, and maturity is an on-going developmental process. While they are in that process, my wife and I see it as part of our job as parents to put up reasonable boundaries and protections around them. If I didn't put internet safety software on our home computer or their iPods, and our kids had a moral failure online, not only would a piece of their innocence be gone, but I would be partly at fault for not having coached them in what to do when they encountered it.

Some would argue that using Internet-restricting software communicates a lack of trust in one's children. Don't fall into this trap. In every area of life there are reasonable boundaries. You don't let your two year old play in the front yard alone when they can't fully grasp the danger of wandering into the street. In your fourteen year old's case, the law has taken the option of driving a car away from your teen. It's not because they will wreck your mini-van if they drive it before they are fifteen. It's because at their age, most have not developed a consistent level of self-control and responsibility to do so.

The reality is that it isn't merely for my teenagers' sake—it is for mine, too. Personally, I am one of more than 75 percent of men that have struggled with Internet pornography. Without going into too much detail, I believe, the ease of accessibility and abundance of Internet pornography is too much for even the most self-disciplined among us. This includes the more than one in three women who struggle with Internet pornography. In the end, it's not about protecting your kids—it's about protecting your whole family.

Finding the Right Software Choice

Internet safety software is used to filter websites to keep out anything inappropriate. There are too many programs out there to review in this space, so I've chosen what I consider the top five. The differences in each isn't in light years, but rather in small degrees. Each is designed to keep out the bad stuff and to provide a reasonable level of safety. They can also be customized to allow you to choose the types of content you want to block or limit with most having thirty or more categories you can prohibit. With most, you also receive instant notification if someone is trying to access something they shouldn't. The average cost of the program is $50 with a year of free updates. The programs will continue to work after that first year, but the database of offensive sites on the web will stop being updated on your system if you fail to update.

Another factor to consider in choosing the right program is your mobile devices. Chances are there are several cell phones, iPods, or tablets in your home. Each one of them should have filtering software on it. For roughly $4.25 a month, this is money well spent.

Teenagers are notorious for letting other people use their devices. Once your child hands someone else their phone, they can no longer control what is looked at or downloaded onto the device. I have several friends whose teens were embarassed after getting back their laptop only to find websites their friend had looked at.

Three of the programs in the chart below have a mobile app that can be downloaded as well. If you are going to use a program that has both a desktop and a mobile app, it will require two separate programs. The easiest thing to do is purchase and install the desktop version first. Then go to the app store for your Apple, Android, or Microsoft device and download straight to your phone or tablet.

Internet Safety Program Comparison Chart

	safeeyes Family Internet Manager	McAfee	Net Nanny	K9 Web	Internet Security Barrier
Pornography	★	★	★	★	★
Online Gaming	★	★	★	–	★
Social Media	★	★	★	★	★
Violence	★	★	★	★	★
Time Controls	★	★	★	★	★
Mobile App	IOS	–	IOS/Android	IOS/Android	–
Alerts/Reports	Instant	Instant	Instant	Online Log	Instant
Mac/Windows	Both	Win	Both	Both	Mac
Cost	$49.95	$49.99	$39.99	FREE	$79.99

Choosing a Gatekeeper

When you set up your software, you'll create a profile for your family. The final step in setting up your profile is to create a username and password. The bearer of the password, or Gatekeeper, is the only person that can make changes to the profile or make exceptions for websites that have been blocked but you want to allow.

If the trap of Internet pornography is part of your own history, then selecting yourself as the Gatekeeper is not the best option. This would be akin to allowing a recovering alcoholic to dispense beer from a keg for the rest of the party. It can be done, but it's not the wisest choice. During the times when pornography had the strongest pull on me, my wife was the Gatekeeper and the only one with the password for all our devices—including my laptop. Yes, it made it inconvenient and awkward at times when websites where blocked that shouldn't be and my wife was the only one that can open them, but it does provide consistent accountability for our family. If pornography has a pull on you, you are putting yourself in dangerous territory by being over confident in your ability to keep your family safe if you can't do it for yourself.

TWEET IT
Setting boundaries for the internet doesn't just protect my child, it protects my whole family.
#techsavvyparent

In some cases, even if online boundaries are a struggle for you, the option of you being the Gatekeeper simply can't be avoided. If this is your situation, then I would recommend an Internet accountability software for yourself that you can find from XXX Church or Convenant Eyes. These programs send a weekly report to an "accountability partner" of everything you've looked at on the web. This way you can keep your family safe as well as yourself.

Keeping Up With Your Mobile Child

Another type of software you should be aware of is social media safety software. This is particularly helpful if you have a young child that is testing the waters of social media such as Pinterest, Instagram, Facebook, etc.

Most social media sites have very little restrictions concerning what can and can not be posted. Social media sites have a two-fold purpose: building community and self-expression. Because of this, young users can tend to go overboard in friending everyone that comes along and they can have poor self-control in knowing what should or shouldn't be posted.

Social media safety software allows you to be able to see what your child is posting, when they are on certain sites, who is on their friend list, and who has sent them messages. This is also a great way to help your child protect their online reputation before anything gets out of hand.

I know you have every intention of checking up on your tween to see what they are doing on each of the sites they frequent, but let's be honest, there is simply not enough hours in the day to keep up. This is the benefit of social media safety software. They can give you a quick snapshot of what your child has been up to on their phone, iPod, Facebook messaging, etc.

Net Nanny has been around for many years and has recently added a social media component to their family protection  programs. Net Nanny Social requires no software. **It is a FREE cloud-based service** that gives you access to your child's social media friends, photos, and videos. It even has a language detector so you can be aware of potential cyberbullying either against your child or from them.

 Social Network Protection from Avira has many of the same features as Net Nanny but has an added friends scan. This feature looks at all of the people on your child's friend list to see who might be out of a safe age range, doesn't have anything in common with your child, or makes inappropriate comments.

 uKnowKids Monitoring from uKnow is a fee-based service, but also more robust than the others. Their program offers not only social media monitoring, but also iPhone and Android cell phone monitoring. One of the best features is the Family Locator Service. You can tag certain places such as school, friend's house, or playground, and uKnowKids will let you know when your child has arrived at one of the destinations.

Regardless of which program you use, keep in mind the purpose isn't to spy on your child's every move. It is to provide safety and accountability. I would caution you about reading every text or post from your child, particularly if they are older. These programs will help bring everything out in to the open, but if your teenager feels you are eavesdropping on her conversations, you run the risk of alienating her and causing her to come up with other ways to communicate with her friends that you may not be aware.

THE DANGEROUS ROULETTE OF VIDEO CHATTING

"Step right up! Step right up," cries the Carney working the midway game at the Fair. He declares that for only one dollar you can spin the giant wheel. "No one is a loser. A winner every time."

Of course, what your eight-year-old is thinking is, "You mean, for only one dollar I can take home a stuffed Bart Simpson toy bigger than me?" The whole experience seems innocent (and inexpensive), but parents recognize it as a deception that is only going to lead to a disappointed child and a temptation to fork over more money for a better result when he doesn't win.

Unfortunately, there is a new kind of roulette in town for teens in which the stakes are much higher and innocence has no part to play. This roulette takes place after school when teens are home alone or during evenings with nothing to do but venture online for a little video chatting.

Through the Peep Hole

Chatting online is not a new thing. It's been around since the early days of AOL when their floppy discs filled our mailboxes. For the most part, people met up in "chat rooms" organized by like interests where strangers could swap celebrity-encounter stories, cooking recipes, or car-restoration ideas.

Video chatting is the next incarnation of online chatting. Unlike texting or IM (instant messaging), there is no anonymity with video chatting. You are always seen by the person with whom you're chatting. Then again, that is the point—to not only be heard but seen. The ease of use and availability have made video chatting very popular with teenagers. It's the feeling of being face-to-face that appeals to teens. Instead of just seeing pictures of your friends on Instagram or Facebook, now you get to talk live to one another.

Virtually all social networking sites now have video chatting integration. Facebook, MySpace, and Google+, all heavily used by teens, allow you to chat with others on their site. This makes it even more important for your teen to know who their online friends are since they can be invited to a video chat by anyone on their friend list. **Recent changes to Google+ even make it possible for a stranger to send you an invite to a video chat without knowing your Gmail.** All the stranger needs is your name. Approximately 41.5% of all teens have a Gmail account. It's

WHERE THE WHEEL STOPS, NOBODY KNOWS!

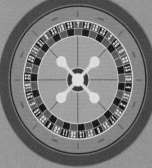

The new generation of chat sites allow you the "thrill" of talking to a different stranger each time you visit the site. Just like a roulette wheel, all you have to do is click "next" to go to your next anonymous encounter.

3 MOST POPULAR VIDEO CHAT SITES

 Omegle chatroulette 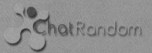 ChatRandom

 Percentage of users on Chatroulette under the age of 30.
It is the largest of all the chat sites.

 ChatRandom's ranking among all chat sites.
It was the fast growing chat site in 2013.

 Percentage of crude behavior and nudity on Chatroulette attributed to men.

 The amount of your personal information that Omegle keeps on their servers and can use in their advertising.
This is the #1 chat app teens are downloading.

YOU THINK IT'S NOT YOUR TEEN?

 Percentage of all teens that use video chat either on the web or through an app.
4 in 10 of all texting teens video chat.

likely that if your child uses email for school that he has a Gmail account. You should be very clear with him about the dangers of responding to a stranger's request on Gmail.

The most popular video chat site/program is Skype. It is widely used by businesses, universities, and even missionaries. My son uses it for an online collaborative class for school. With Skype you only get to talk with people that are on your contact list. There is no talking to random strangers. Because of this built-in security measure, Skype is not only the most popular, but the most legitimate and safe. Once you move past Skype, however, the video-chatting waters become a bit murky.

Other popular chat sites, such as ChatRoulette and Bazoocam are more insidious in that neither site requires a login name or password in order to chat. When you launch the site, you are simply asked to give permission for the site to turn on your webcam. When you click "start," the camera comes on and you begin to chat live on video with a random participant—Roulette wheel fashion—in

Who's Doing all the Video Chatting?

33% of Guys

42% of Girls

27% have created their own videos and uploaded to YouTube or Facebook.

Resource: Pew Research Center's Internet & American Life Teen/Parent Survey, Apr. 2010.

France, Iceland, the Ukraine, or any other place in the world. According to a study done by the office of the Texas Attorney General, "Nearly half of the randomly selected users encountered by Cyber Crimes investigators immediately exposed themselves and conducted sexually explicit acts on camera." Another study by RJMetrics concluded that **1 in 8 chats on these sites will yield something "R Rated"** and that 23% of females participating on the site are under the age of twenty.

The Illusion of Anonymity

We've already mentioned that with video chatting you can always see the person with whom you are chatting. Yet teens still think this qualifies as anonymous. One girl explaining why she uses Chat Roulette commented, "I like being able to meet new guys and it be completely anonymous." But wait. If you can see the other person, and they can see you...huh? Perhaps she means anonymous in the sense that none of her real-life friends will find out about the creeps she talks to online.

As always, it is important to realize that nothing is ever strictly private or anonymous online. The same is true of video chatting. While video chats can be conducted with a measure of safety when you know and trust the person you are chatting with, **teens should be mindful that anything they say or show in a video chat can be recorded and used by the other person, sometimes for illegal purposes.**

Thus far teens haven't shown great discretion with their supposed anonymity in other uses of technology. In a 2009 study by The National Campaign to Prevent Teen and Unplanned Pregnancy, 20% of teens say that they have sent/posted nude or semi-nude pictures or videos of themselves. Furthermore, 39% say they have sent sexually suggestive text messages to another person. I would be willing to bet that those teens assumed that their picture or video was only going to be seen by the person to whom it was sent—like a secret or a private prank. **It never enters their mind that the other person they are video chatting or swapping sexy photos with can record the video or use those photos against them later.** This is exactly what happened in 2009 when a nineteen-year-old man posed as a girl on Facebook. His deception convinced more than 30 male classmates to send nude photos and videos of themselves. In exchange she (he) would do the same. He then used the photos/videos to blackmail his classmates into performing oral sex.

WATCH OUT

Make sure your child knows that any video chat they take part in can be captured by the other person.

Teens also have a difficult time seeing how their cyber actions can affect real world perceptions others have of them: 40% of girls said they sent sexually suggestive messages "as a joke" or to be funny, but 39% of recipients said that they perceived the sexual text as a real-world expectation to hookup or date. Did you get that? What a teenager may intent as "good fun," the stranger on the other end could perceive as a sexual invite.

Researchers from Simon Fraser University recently did a study concerning teens and their use of video chatting. One of the areas of interest in the study was the sexual content of teen video chatting.

Some teens in the study said that the longer the video conversation went the more likely they were to "show some skin." Some teens went so far as to say that they would masturbate while the other person watching would do the same. One teen boy said, "I've had some friends who intentionaly go naked on Skype just to liven up the conversation." Another guy remarked that "sex talk is easier with video because you can see each other."[1]

Video chatting is further normalizing nudity as an everyday part of the teen experience, much like internet pornography has done before it. The constant and repeated exposure causes teens to lose any sense of shock or shame when it comes to nudity or self-exposure.

Saying "No" to Spinning the Wheel

It may be fun to go to the fair and spin the wheel in hopes of taking home a giant panda bear, but letting your teen take chances with strangers online is in no way safe. There can be legitimate benefits to video chatting if it is done in a controlled environment with mature participants and accountability. If video chatting is going to be a part of your teen's experience, here are a few things to discuss.

1. **Parents Go First.** Before saying "no" to video chatting, check it out yourself. Set up your own account and get on the sites your teen wants to use. If you say "yes," then they'll know it's because you found it to be safe. If you say "no," then they will know you are making an informed decision. Either way you've covered your bases as the parent.

2. **Chat in the Open.** Any video chatting should be done in an open place in your home that will provide accountability for your teen and for the other participants. Letting your teenager video chat in their bedroom is only asking for trouble and moral failure.

3. **No Strangers Allowed.** To be as safe as possible, video chatting should be strictly with people your teen knows personally or has known for some time on a friend list.

4. **No Place for Sexy.** Many teens feel that being "sexy" online is an accepted flirting practice. But once you open the door to sexy, it's a difficult one to close. Provocative dress and language should be absolutely forbidden. At present, there are several states that are enacting cyber-sex laws regarding minors.

TWEET IT Letting your teenager video chat online is like spinning a roulette wheel with nothing but trouble as the outcome. #techsavvyparent

5. **Personal Should Remain Personal.** Your teen should avoid giving out personal information during a chat session. Because of the intimate nature of a video chat, it's more tempting to share personal info. You feel like you know the other person since you can see one another, but formal rules of communication should still apply.

Cyberbullying: It's all the rage

Every playground has one. When I was in elementary school there was one kid that would reign terror in the hearts of all of us skinny boys. He would regularly toss one of us off of the swing set or push a little too hard during tag. If he had a football in his hand, you knew better than to get near him lest you became his newest tackling dummy.

All it took to shake us in our boots, was for him to walk up to one of us, stare menacingly in our eyes and announce, "Hey you, after school; you and me by the monkey bars." It was like a scene out of the movie *Sandlot*.

One fall day, it was my turn to be the object of his aggression. I remember the fear of thinking, "I'll never see sixth grade. There is no way one of my friends can help. I dare not tell a teacher or it will only get worse." You better believe I didn't show up at the monkey bars that afternoon.

On that day in fifth grade, I knew what my bully looked like, I knew where he sat in lunch, and I knew his name. The difference with bullying today is that many times the bully is on a computer screen or phone and is completely anonymous. This means that if your child is a victim, he or she may walk the halls of the school suspecting everyone they see. Imagine the paralyzing feeling of your daughter not knowing who keeps sending the text that says, "You fat, Ho. We wish you weren't here." Maybe your son keeps getting a post on his Instagram that says, "You boy lover, if you were dead no one would care." This is the trauma that thousands of children and teenagers feel every day. **The constant ridicule causes as many as 160,000 students to skip school each day.**[1]

Cyberbullying is such a new issue that we didn't even have a term for it until a few years ago. But with the proliferation of screens in our children's lives the harassment has moved from the playground to their bedroom. It is the intentional harassment or demeaning of an individual for their religious views, body size, sexual orientation, gender, or family background. It is the practice of attacking another person by means of technology simply for being themselves.

The majority of teenagers believe adults don't take cyberbullying seriously enough. It could be that most adults have no regular contact with teenagers and don't realize how damaging cyberbullying can be. After all, isn't it just picking on someone? That's the kind of thing that's been taking place in every generation of teenagers. But cyberbullying is different. It's much more than pushing someone in the hall. It is a persistent attack that can quickly grow from one person to a mob and can happen on so many different fronts that the victim sees no way out. Take a look at this list of ways cyberbullying can manifest:

- Sending mean or threatening messages to a person's email or cell phone.

- Spreading rumors online or through mass texting.

- Posting threatening messages on social media.

- Stealing a person's account information to post lies on her profile page as if she said them.

- Pretending to be someone else online to threaten or harass another person.

- Taking unflattering pictures of someone and passing them around by cell phone or social media.

- Sending a sexually related photo or message about someone.

Why Bullies Bully

Bullying has always been rooted in one person trying to show his or her dominance or control over someone else. We've all seen the stereotype bully in a movie that takes the lunch money from a smaller kid or gives a wedgie in the locker room. Cyberbullying is far more sinister and psychologically traumatizing. **Right at 58% of cyberbullies said the reason why they did it was because the other person deserved it.** From the bully's perspective, there is something wrong with the other person—a flaw that makes them less deserving of respect and kindness.

In the case of a twelve year old from Hardy, Arkansas, Sarah Lynn Butler's "flaw" was that she was voted queen of the town's upcoming Fall Festival. Soon afterwards, girls at her school began posting messages on social media calling her a "slut." The last message she received said, "No one will miss you when you are gone." While at home that day, Sarah took her life.

For fifteen-year-old Phoebe Prince, the issue that made her a target for bullies was that she was an immigrant. After a relationship with a boy at school ended badly, the bullying from other girls started. She was called "Irish slut" and "whore" on Twitter, Facebook, and Formspring. After months of relentless cyberbullying, Phoebe took her life. Even after her death, girls from her school continued to post hateful comments on her Facebook memorial page.

Fourteen-year-old Kenneth Weishuhn Jr. became the focus of attacks after he told friends he was gay. These "friends" turned on him and began sending death threats to his cell phone. The attacks continued online as boys at his school setup a Gay Hate Group on Facebook and posted Kenneth's picture on the group.

These are just three of the dozens of victims that had been bullied online so intently and unrelentingly that they saw no way to end the

THE BULLIES & WHO THEY BULLY

The most common victims of cyberbullying?

1. 16-17 yr old girls

2. Homosexual Teens

3. Teens with Disabilities

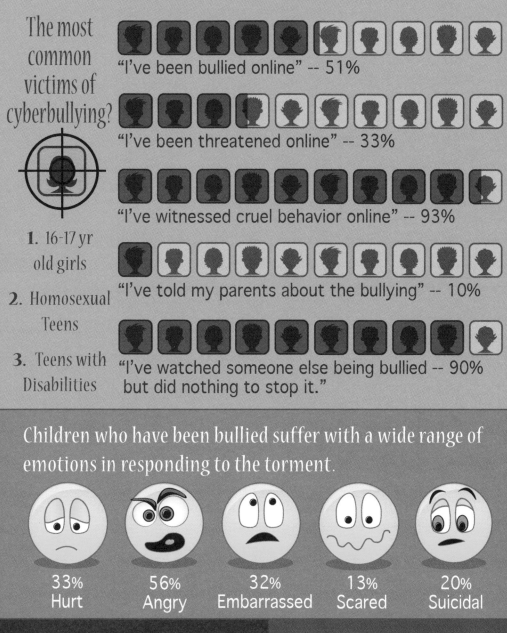

"I've been bullied online" -- 51%

"I've been threatened online" -- 33%

"I've witnessed cruel behavior online" -- 93%

"I've told my parents about the bullying" -- 10%

"I've watched someone else being bullied -- 90% but did nothing to stop it."

Children who have been bullied suffer with a wide range of emotions in responding to the torment.

| 33% Hurt | 56% Angry | 32% Embarrassed | 13% Scared | 20% Suicidal |

"CYBERBULLYING IS THE MOST COMMON ONLINE RISK FOR ALL TEENS."
American Academy of Pediatrics

Girls are more than twice as likely as boys to BE BULLIED & to BE BULLIES!

Source: Bureau of Justice Statistics, US Department of Health and Human Services, Cyberbullying Research Center; www.AAP.org.

abuse other than to end their lives.

The other reason why teenagers take part in cyberbullying is for pleasure. **Another 28% of cyberbullies said the reason why they caused the abuse was because it was entertaining.** There is a sadistic nature to cyberbullying, perhaps because it is rarely one individual to another. It quickly spreads like a virus with the instigator pulling in many other students to pile on the abuse. Before you know it, it is no longer a singular cyberbully but a cybermob that develops.

Looking for the Signs

The destructive nature of cyberbullying can cause victims to feel weak, vulnerable, and violated. Children attacked online can easily spiral into depression and a self-destructive pattern. Contemplating suicide is a horrific option, yet 20% of all bullied victims have done so. According to a British study in 2013, half of all teen suicides are related to bullying.

Young teens' feelings about their position in social circles—what others say about them and how their peers view them—shapes how they see their own self worth. When their "friends" turn on them and say things such as, "Everyone hates you," "We wish you were dead," and "We all only pretend to like you," they internalize those words. They must find some way to deal with the pain. Unfortunately for many bullied children, the way to express the pain is through actions that hurt themselves even more.

Be watchful for some of the following behaviors from your child. If you see a pattern, it doesn't necessarily mean they are being bullied but at the very least there is a problem that should be addressed.

- Reluctance to attend school
- Ongoing trouble sleeping
- Abruptly walking away from computer
- Declining grades
- Suicidal thoughts or attempts
- Withdrawal from friends
- Suddenly stops using computer, video games, social media, etc.

If Your Child is Being Bullied

As a parent, when you find out someone has threatened your child in some way the tendency is to go "Momma Bear" all over the situation. If you are a dad, maybe you turn into Super Man and think you can make all of this go away. Unfortunately, dealing with a cyberbully takes a little more nuance and strategy, rather than a frontal assault.

Most of us have a memory of being on the playground and being pushed by someone bigger than us. If it was more than an isolated incident, maybe you went so far as to tell a parent or teacher. We all pretty much got the same advice back then. "If they push you again, you need to push them back...just once, then they'll see they can't do that to you," was the standard response from dad. He wasn't necessarily giving permission to fight, but rather the freedom to retaliate if needed.

WATCH OUT

Not taking bullying seriously can make your child feel isolated and defenseless. Even if your child is partly to blame, they need your support to bring it to an end.

Dealing with a cyberbully is radically different than a playground push or teasing in the hallway. **Responding online to a cyberbully is the absolute worst thing to do to make the abuse stop.** Replying (in words) to a cyberbully does two things. One, it lets the bully know that your child actually received the message. Without a response, she never gets the satisfaction of knowing your child saw the message. Once she knows the account is active, more messages typically flood in. Two, if your child responds with a message back to the bully, now the bully has your child's own words to use against them later. Those words get spread or misquoted. Copy, edit, paste, and repeat.

More than likely, the person(s) instigating the cyberbullying is a peer of your child's that they know—a classmate, sports teammate, former boyfriend/girlfriend, or even a disgruntled best friend. The last thing you want is to lose emotional control by going toe-to-toe with one of your child's friends. As much as you may want the bullying to stop, responding to the messages online will only make things worse for your child and possibly put you at legal risk for harassment. Instead of retaliating, here are steps to stop the bullying and hold the person accountable. Read each of these with your child.

- Ð Take a screenshot of every offending message immediately. Afterwards delete the messages or photos from your social media profiles. Then BLOCK THE PERSON'S PROFILE.

- Ð Date and file the messages in case you need them for the authorities later. In the meantime, do not look at them again. It will only serve to fill your heart and mind with hurtful lies.

- Ð Do not retaliate online with harsh words yourself. Responding to the bully will inflame the situation. The bully could distort or distribute your words to others.

- Ð If the attacks occurred on a social networking site, report the harassment to the site administrator or help center. Each of the following links can show you how to make a report. It usually doesn't take very long for the company to act.
  - Facebook.com/help
  - support.twitter.com
  - help.instagram.com

- Ð Tell an adult that will act on your behalf. Your school, sports teams, place of employment, and even social media sites have policies against cyberbullying.

- Ð If the bullying involves threat of physical or sexual assault, you must contact your local authorities immediately. Once cyberbullying escalates, it usually does not stop until the authorities get involved. This many sound extreme, but you have the right to **NOT BE** harassed. Let them help you.

- Ð   As a last step, be willing to setup new social networking, email, and cell phone accounts. This is inconvenient, but keep your eye on the big picture of freeing yourself from the continued abuse.

The Law of the Land

For more than a year, twelve-year-old Rebecca Sedwick was tormented by bullies on Facebook and her cell phone. Another classmate even urged her to just "drink bleach and die." Even after

THE SILENT VICTIMS

ONLY 1 IN 10 BULLIED VICTIMS EVER TELL ANYONE. 58% HAVE NEVER TOLD AN ADULT ABOUT WHAT HAPPENED TO THEM.

ONLY 7% OF PARENTS SAY THEY ARE WORRIED ABOUT CYBERBULLYING, BUT 33% OF TEENS SAY THEY HAVE BEEN BULLIED. 85% OF BULLIED TEENS SAID THEIR SCHOOL DIDN'T HELP ENOUGH TO STOP THE PROBLEM FROM RECURRING.

MORE THAN 3 MILLION SCHOOL ABSENCES EACH MONTH ARE ATTRIBUTED TO BULLYING.

Source: Cyberbullyhotline.com, 2012 · DoSomething.org/11-tips-about-cyberbullying; www.bullyingstatistics.org

pulling Rebecca from her public school in favor of home schooling, the attacks didn't stop. Feeling there was no way to end the bullying, Rebecca climbed to the top of an abandoned building and jumped to her death.

After her death, the attacks didn't stop. Her tormentor posted the following on Rebecca's Facebook page. **"Yes IK (I know) I bullied Rebecca and she killed herself but IDGAF (I don't give a f***)."** Because of a new cyberbullying law in Florida, this online unremorseful admission led to an arrest of her fourteen-year-old attacker. She and another girl were both charged with a felony. Ten years ago not a single state had a law in regard to cyberbullying. This isn't surprising since no one was aware of the long term damaging effects it was having on teens and tweens.

TWEET IT
As parents it's our job to protect our kids from cyber-bullying. If you think it's happening, ask. They'll love you for it. #techsavvyparent

Today, 39 states have laws outlawing cyberharassment and another 37 have laws on the books punishing cyber-stalking. These apply primarily to the actions of legal adults. Only 19 states have laws specifically banning cyberbullying that apply to minors. Another five states have proposed laws that have not yet passed. Almost all 50 states have policies that require public schools to address issues of bullying and cyberbullying. To see if your state has a law regarding cyberbullying, visit online at www.cyberbullying.us.

Regardless if there is legal leverage to help protect your child from being bullied, the first line of defense is always you as a parent. If you suspect your child is being bullied, they may feel too helpless to verbalize it to you. Before jumping in to fix the situation, take the time to build them back up again. The most important thing right now is for them to know you are in their corner and you think highly of them.

THE ALLURE OF
INTERNET PORNOGRAPHY

The Sesame Street YouTube Channel has more than 850,000 subscribers. This doesn't include the millions of others who merely visit the channel to watch videos of Elmo, Grover, Big Bird, and the rest of the gang. On any ordinary day, it would be a great opportunity for little kids to watch video clips from the PBS program to hone their reading skills, practice their multiplication tables, or learn positive life lessons. But October 16, 2011, would not be that day.

Instead of the usual children's content, hackers replaced the channel's videos with those of explicit pornography. The brazen hacker left a mocking message that in part read, "WHO DOESN'T LOVE PORN, KIDS? RIGHT! EVERYONE LOVES IT! AND WE'RE GONNA MAKE ALL OF AMERICA HAPPY!"

It took less than half an hour for YouTube to be notified, and for the offending videos to be removed. But the damage had already been done. No, not the reputation of PBS. This wasn't their fault. The damage was to the minds of the children who clicked a picture expecting to see Cookie Monster and instead had a whole new world opened up to them.

Some would say that it's really not that big of a deal. Some would say that it's a rite of passage—that in today's culture it's just going to happen. But doesn't that put childhood exposure to pornography on the level as no more traumatic than getting a cavity or discovering there is no Easter Bunny?

I can still remember the first time I saw a pornographic image. I don't merely remember when it happened, I remember what it looked like. That first image was more than thirty years ago, and it's still with me today. It will never go away.

That first image led to more images and a stronger pull toward the forbidden. Whether single or married, I struggled for years wanting to know why the distortion of God's design for sexuality was digging its claws into me. In his song, "Everybody Medicates," Ross King sings the following:

> *He looks at pictures on the Internet*
> *He needs it much more than he should*
> *He's surprised no one has caught him yet*
> *He wishes someone would*

7 Facts you didn't know about internet pornography

1. 12% of all websites are pornographic

2. 25% of all search engine requests are for PORN.

Search Celebrities
Search Directions
Search Recipes
Search PORN

3. $3075 is being spent on porn EVERY SECOND.

4. The state with the most subscribers to paid porn sites is Utah.

9 of the top 10 states are conservative states

We're #1

5. 2.5 BILLION EMAIL sent each day are related to pornography.

6. The day of the year with the least amount of porn activity:

Thanksgiving

7. Sunday is the most popular day of the week for viewing porn.

REASONS WHY TEENS VIEWED INTERNET PORNOGRAPHY	
Wanted the Sexual Excitement	**69.3%**
Curious about Things People Do Sexually	**53.1%**
Wanted Information about Sex	**39.7%**
With Friends Who Wanted to Look at It	**34.1%**

Source: The Nature and Dynamics of Internet Pornography Exposure for Youth, CyberPsychology & Behavior, Volume 11, Number 6, 2008.

Believe me, it's the same thing your son or daughter is thinking as they look at pornography. They don't like how it makes them feel about themselves. Deep down they want to stop, but they don't know how. It's not something they'll simply "get over," and it's important for you as a parent to understand how it happens in the first place.

Why Teenagers are Drawn to Porn

Our sexual identity is at the core of who we are. It didn't take too long playing tag on the school playground before we recognized there was a difference between boys and girls. For many of us, when we got to our late elementary years, we developed our first crushes. You can remember when that boy or girl came by your table in the cafeteria and you got nervous, couldn't breathe well, or think straight. Then you hit early middle school and everything in your body started changing. We all went through this uncomfortable, yet natural, stage of our bodies maturing.

During this time in puberty, for both guys and girls, there becomes a curiosity with the body. Who could blame them—everything in their bodies is seemingly changing overnight? Their bodies are growing up and out, developing pimples and zits, putting off foul odors, and developing hair in new places. It all seems so foreign to them. And in the midst of all of this, for the first time their changing bodies become attractive to one another.

Any sociologist or child development expert can tell you that this attraction comes because children are moving from childhood into a time where their bodies are preparing for sexual reproduction. Young teenagers have a thousand questions about what is happening to and in their bodies. Many of these questions revolve around sexual intercourse and sexual activities. Unfortunately, most of their questions aren't verbalized. But when they start asking questions, whether they verbalize them or not, they are going to try and find answers.

Unfortunately, the first place teens and tweens (9-12 year olds) go to to find help with sexual curiosity is the Internet, more specifically, good old Google. The first time most young tweens view pornography is either by accident or out of curiosity. In a study out of Penn State Harrisburg published in *CyberPsychology & Behavior*,

NUMBER OF TIMES TEEN BOYS ADMIT TO VIEWING EACH TYPE OF INTERNET PORNOGRAPHY	
Naked People but No Sexual Activity	18 TIMES
Naked People Showing Genitals	16.5 TIMES
Sexual Intercourse with a Man/Woman	16.7 TIMES
Sexual Intercourse Involving a Group	12.5 TIMES
Sexual Intercourse with Same Sex	11.1 TIMES

Source: The Nature and Dynamics of Internet Pornography Exposure for Youth, CyberPsychology & Behavior, Volume 11, Number 6, 2008.

researchers found that more than half were curious about sexual activities while another four in ten were simply looking for information about sex.[1] Don't misunderstand. I'm not excusing even the first exposure. I'm merely saying I can see how it happens. However, it's what follows after the first exposure that is more troubling.

Each year the porn industry makes more money than all MLB, NBA, NHL, & NFL teams combined.

PORN $$$$ >

The same Penn State study, and many others, show that viewing pornography doesn't stop after the first incident. The initial curiosity gives way to a desire for pleasure. **Nearly 70% of teens who look at pornography admit they enjoy the sexual excitement it brings.** From there it is difficult to control or to stop. Among those who have viewed porn, most have viewed videos involving sexual intercourse at least sixteen times and seen group sexual activities more than a dozen times. There may be shame after the fact, but guys are willing to suppress it because of the immediately sexual satisfaction.

Recently my daughter came home with a treat from the grocery store. It was a giant tub of cheese balls. We love cheese balls, but these were an off-brand we had never heard of. We hurriedly ripped the lid off and popped a few into our mouths. It was then we discovered why they were so inexpensive. They tasted AWFUL! But a funny thing happened. After a few minutes we tried another one, you know, just to make sure we were right. Sure enough, it tasted awful as well. Over the course of the next two hours, we must have eaten a hundred of those blasted things.

No matter how many times we ate them, they were still unsatisfying. They tasted artificial and unnatural, but they also had just a hint of real cheese. It was enough of an authentic flavor that we couldn't help but keep eating. Pornography is the same way.

I have worked with teenagers for more than two decades, and I have yet to meet a teenaged young man who said, "I used to look at porn, but I decided I didn't want to anymore and quit." Porn has just enough resemblance and satisfaction to the real thing that you *almost* can't help but keep coming back. If your teenager is viewing porn, he won't simply decide to stop. As he gets older, the pressure and opportunity to look is only going to get greater.

How Porn Changed the Dorm

Over Christmas break, I talked to a recent high school graduate who is now attending the college of his dreams. This is an experience that he has worked toward for the last four years. He was solidly plugged into his church youth group and came from a strongly religious family. Now that he has ventured out on his own, I was curious how the opportunity was shaping up for him. He said, "I love my classes and I love my new friends. There is just one thing I was unprepared for." "What's that?" I questioned. I wasn't prepared for the bluntness of his answer or aggitation in his voice.

Gratingly, he continued, "You can never get away from porn. It is literally everywhere. When I walk into my dorm room, my roommate has it on his laptop. If I walk down the hall, just about every room has it on. I can't even go to the guy's commons area because they watch it out in the open whenever there aren't girls around."

I wish this was an atypical situation, but I'm afraid it is commonplace today. **This is the first generation of teens to grow up with porn readily available for FREE whenever they want it.** It is bound to change their perceptions of

How **PORN** affects your child

93% of boys & **62%** of girls have been exposed to internet pornography **BEFORE THE AGE OF 18.**

70% of boys have spent more than 30 minutes at a time looking at internet porn.

83% of boys & **57%** of girls have seen **GROUP SEX** on the internet.

71% of teens hide their online activities from their parents.

US counties with the highest percentage of teens have the highest click rate for internet porn.

Is your child looking at **PORN**?

Each statement that is true of you increases the likelihood that your child is looking at internet porn

I live in an urban community.

I make an above average income.

I regularly volunteer in my community.

I have a college degree.

I am conservative in my religious beliefs.

their own sexuality and how they interact with others.

In an earlier chapter we looked at some of the figures from the Sex and Tech Survey regarding teens and how they express their sexuality through technology. The numbers go even higher for college age students:[2]

Ð **67%** OF YOUNG MEN AND **49%** OF YOUNG WOMEN SAY THAT VIEWING PORN IS AN ACCEPTABLE WAY TO EXPRESS ONE'S SEXUALITY.

Ð **64%** OF COLLEGE GUYS AND **18%** OF COLLEGE WOMEN SPEND TIME ONLINE FOR INTERNET SEX **EVERY WEEK**.

Ð **31%** OF COLLEGE GUYS AND **36%** OF COLLEGE GIRLS HAVE POSTED NUDE/SEMI-NUDE IMAGES OF THEMSELVES ONLINE.

Ð **21%** OF THE WOMEN AND **30%** OF THE MEN WHO POSTED SEXUAL PICTURES OF THEMSELVES SENT THEM TO SOMEONE THEY WANTED TO DATE OR HOOK UP WITH.

Behaviors such as binge drinking, marijuana usage, and uncommitted sex all peak around age 22. A new study from Brigham Young University shows that viewing internet porn doesn't follow the same pattern. In other words, once you start looking at porn you don't really "grow out of it."

Your Response is a Key to Prevention

It's not uncommon to walk into your son's room and see the screen on his laptop suddenly change or be quickly closed as if he's hiding something. We've had that experience with both of our children. It doesn't mean there was necessarily something wrong, but it does give a parent cause for concern. Maybe you've already had worse happen when you sat down at your home computer to do a Google search. As you type in a few keystrokes, the search engine does an autofill of what it thinks you are looking for and without warning the words "nude college girls" pops up on your screen. When you take a look at the internet history, your heart sinks. A wave of emotions flood over you: shock, anger, disbelief, sadness. And all of them are appropriate.

Next comes the even more difficult task—talking with your son or daughter.

If you are a mom, your gut tells you to take the computer, smash it against the wall, ground him until next year, and scream, "How dare you bring this into my home!" But if you do, then you both lose. He misses out on seeing his parent care for him in the midst of a breached boundary. You lose the opportunity to have a meaningful, mature, potentially relationship-changing conversation with your son. Now that it is out in the open that he is looking at porn, you know he's ready for some answers about sex, and there is no one better to have this conversation with him than his mom or dad.

The most important thing is to remain calm. If your child is younger, then responding with shock and an incredulous tone can easily communicate that sex itself is a bad thing. He's already confused about sex as it is. He doesn't need for his mom or dad to give the impression that sex (within God's design) is a dirty or bad thing.

Remember, if he is young, chances are either he was looking for information or it happened by accident. The typical boy's first exposure to internet porn is age eleven. It is almost always by accident. More than 26 different children's cartoon character names are linked to thousands of pornographic pages. Your child could have been searching for Pokemon, but came upon something altogether different. What he needs now is your help, not your shock.

Likewise, NEVER use shame as a deterrent. Regardless of the age at which it happens, if you find that your teenager is viewing pornography, shame and humiliation are never a good way to handle the situation. He already feels embarrassed about it, but calling him a "pervert" or "sick" will almost guarantee that he will continue to struggle and will do so even more in the dark. Shame causes us to move into darkness because we don't want anyone to see us. You can still express disappointment with his decision, but you wish he would have first talked to you for answers.

At some point in your conversation with your child, calmly explain why pornography is a distortion of God's design for sex. When should sexual intercourse take place? Why did God give us the gift of sex? Your son should also understand that much of pornography is dehumanizing to the women involved and many of them (even here in America) are in a form of sexual slavery. It communicates that women are only valuable to the degree to which they can sexually gratify men.

It is best that your child, whether a guy or a girl, has these conversations with both mom and dad. I recognize that in many families that is simply not possible. If you are a single mom, please allow me to speak into your situation for a moment. If you are a single dad, you can apply this as needed. My heart feels for you in having to raise a child on your own. Having conversations about sexuality is never easy and is only compounded when you have to go it alone. But your teen needs you (and trusts you) more than anyone else. He knows this is uncomfortable for you to talk about, too.

As a mom, you have an opportunity to be the one woman in his life who can share with him what it means to value a woman for her true beauty. You get to help him see how to cherish and honor a woman by the way he treats you. Share with him the hopes you have for him when it comes to healthy friendships, dating, and marriage. He may not know how to say it now, but he will benefit from those conversations with you for the rest of his life.

Taking Bold Steps to Protect Their Heart

Here are a few steps your family can take together to begin addressing pornography before the temptation happens and to create a family plan so all of your family is protected.

1. **Start Talking About it at a Young Age.** The average age of a child's first exposure to internet porn is nine. Either you can act like it will never affect your child or you can prepare them for when it is likely to happen. A child can't understand pornography, but he can understand why we don't look at people without their clothes on. Bring it down to his level and assure him that if a picture of a person without their clothes on ever pops up on the computer, he should tell you immediately.

2. **Explain God's Design for Sex.** Too many times kids have a negative view of sex or even their own sexuality because parents don't take the time to talk with them about it. As they get older, they should be told the context in which sex should take place. It's not a one-time talk to have. It's an ongoing conversation you have at an age-appropriate level. Porn is always outside of God's design for how we should be sexually satisfied.

3. **Communicate Clear Boundaries.** Your teen needs to hear from you that pornography is never an acceptable way to learn about sexuality or to satisfy our curiosity. You don't have to be mean about it to communicate that pornography is not permissible in your home. If he continues to struggle with this boundary, it may be necessary to remove the temptation by keeping him off the computer, iPhone, or tablet for a period of time. This will give him a pause to relearn self-control in this area of life.

4. **Establish Barriers for Protection.** Just because you are now talking openly with your teen about this issue doesn't mean you can solely leave it up to his self-discipline. I've learned from my own struggles that I can't always manage in this area, so I don't expect my son to either. If you don't have an Internet Safety program installed on ALL of your computers, then do it NOW! Having Internet Safety software such as K9 Web Protection or Content Barrier can help in protecting your child's heart and mind.

5. **Share Your Own Journey.** Don't let your son think he is the only one who deals with this. This is particularly true if you are a dad. You know your own struggles with this temptation. Let him know that since you understand, you won't let him deal with this on his own. At an age-appropriate level, he needs to know some of your own journey in dealing with this issue.

6. **Be the Accountability He Will Value.** Your teenager is going to have moral failures, and if this is the area of his life where it will happen, he will need your help. The only way he will come to you is if you make it safe for him. If he gets up enough courage to talk to you about his struggles, then you need to receive him with grace and be ready to help. You can be his biggest advocate for spiritual, relational, and emotional health. Holding him accountable for his choices doesn't mean you should not also extend grace. Figure out a balance for yourself by asking other parents how they have dealt with this issue.

Girls and Pornography

While it's true that boys look at pornography sooner and more often, girls still fall prey to the allure of pornography as well. The curiosity in early adolescence with sex and sexual activities happens with both boys and girls. The study from Penn State Harrisburg showed that 62.1% of girls before eighteen had seen internet porn.

Most girls struggle with their body image—how they see themselves physically. Girls know that most adolescent boys look at internet porn and the women in the videos become the standard of beauty. They can be drawn to pornography out of a sense of longing for the perfect body or to be the object of male attention.

Teen girls are fed with a constant diet from our culture that their bodies make them who they are. More than 80% of girls report feeling pressure from media to diet or to look thinner. The books they read, magazines they flip through, and teen-oriented TV programs they watch all tell them that they have to be "sexy" in order for boys to notice them. They feel they aren't tall enough, tan enough, skinny enough, or buxom enough—all of which are lies.

If you have a daughter, she needs to hear from you each day that she has great worth. Don't let pop culture or the internet take away from your daughter the joy of being who God made her to be.

CONCLUSION

My own children are teenagers, and technology is every bit a part of their lives as it is in your own child's. My wife and I struggle each day to help our two teens find balance in their lives. We want them to be able to use screens well. We just don't want it to define who they are or to block out other more important pursuits such as friendships, family, faith, and their future.

For all parents, one of the most difficult aspects of monitoring technology in our kids' lives is that it changes so fast. It is difficult to keep up. Just when you feel like you've mastered the ins and outs of a Nintendo Wii, they go and release a new system. You replace your own cell phone only to find the new one has twenty-eight new wingdings. After a year of using it, you still haven't figured out all of these new "must have" features. It's enough to drive any parent crazy. And it does me, too.

You've experienced the whiplash of trying to keep up with your middle schooler's ever-changing food preferences, clothing styles, mood swings, romantic crushes, and school projects. At the end of the day, you find it difficult to let your mind and body rest because you're still trying to make sense of it all and make the right choice for your child. Grasping at straws, you just want to know if you still have any relevance in their life, or if all of their "stuff" has taken your place. Don't feel foolish. I'm right there with you.

> **GOOD NEWS**
> The majority of teenagers say the person(s) they most admire in life is their parents.

In those moments of doubt, confusion, or flat out exhaustion, it is easy to give up and just let it go. It makes you feel like your teenager doesn't value your direction or you've lost influence in their life. But don't give up! No matter how you feel at the moment, **the reality is you are the greatest influence in the life of your child.**

Study after study has shown that even though your impressionable teen may respect her coach, may love her teacher, may gravitate toward a church small group leader—all pale in comparison to the influence you possess. Your teen may not know how to verbalize it, but you are the one on the highest pedestal. A study conducted by MTV and the Associated Press asked teenagers these two questions: (1) Who in your life do you most admire? (2) With whom do you most enjoy spending time? The answer to both questions by a majority of teenagers was...drum roll..."My parents." So take a deep breath, and keep at it. Here a few pointers to keep yourself sharp as a parent.

1. **Keep Reading and Learning.** Don't get discouraged that you don't know everything about technology. You never will...and neither will I. It all changes too quickly to keep up with it. Instead of feeling overwhelmed or defeated, start small. Begin by reading one tech-related blog or article each week. For starters, try out TUAW, TechCrunch, engadget, CultofAndroid, or CNetNews.

2. **Keep the Dialogue Open.** Your children, teens in particular, are going to have broken boundaries and moral failures. Even when they disappoint, don't relationally close the door on them. Make sure they know you will always receive them and that your love is not based on their obedience. Creating this kind of relationship will increase the odds that you are the one they will want to talk to when they do fail.

3. **Remember the End Game.** Don't lose sight of what your goal is for your teenager. It may seem to them (and you at times) that all you do is say "no" to your teenager's plea for more technology freedom or to bend the rules. But the goal isn't to have an obedient child or even one that is adept at technology. The goal is to develop a responsible person who makes choices in life that are honoring of themselves and those around them. Make sure you incorporate your heart into your ongoing conversation with your teen, as well as affirm the person you see them becoming, not just their right behavior.

4. **Don't Back Down.** If your decisions are not arbitrary, then you should never feel pressure to lower your standards. Proper boundaries are a good thing. Just make sure that if you have a boundary when it comes to who they can talk to online, when they can play video games, or when they can get their first cell phone, that you can also clearly explain why. Your teenager may not agree with your rule, but they will respect your clear thinking and willingness to take time to explain.

5. **Talk to Other Parents.** Teenagers are geniuses at making parents feel isolated. Your teenager loves you, but at just the right moment he can also make you feel like you are the only parent out there with rules. Share with other parents what you are learning about technology and ask them to do the same for you. You'll begin to see that all of us are struggling with these issues. Talking to other parents can also keep your own actions in check when you might be overreacting in a situation with your kid. The goal of this journey was not only to make you a tech savvy parent, but a more confident, balanced, and loving one as well.

Create a Theology of Technology

I want to close by talking for a moment about why I am passionate about all of this. I am keenly aware of my own struggles of the flesh and the destruction that the misuse of technology can bring to my family. I also know that the only hope I have of maintaining a relationally and emotionally healthy family is because my sins have been paid for by Jesus Christ.

I am in the spiritual process of being transformed into the image of Christ. And my family is being transformed as well. We are on a spiritual journey together to honor God with our lives. Some days are much more difficult than others, but I have the assurance that I am not in this alone as a parent. Christ is with me.

I realize you may not embrace the same religious beliefs as me, and I am not here to judge that. But since my faith in Christ is paramount to who my family is, it is a compass that determines how we live as a family. If you are a follower of Christ, I hope you too see these principles as a theology of sorts for how your family can use technology. If you are not a part of the Christian faith, I hope you can still see these as healthy principles that can guide the boundaries you set for your family.

Seeking After Solitude

"If you look for me in earnest, you will find me when you seek me."

Jeremiah 29.13

The typical teenager spend 11.5 hours each day connected to some form of media. From the time they get up they are bombarded with stimuli that rarely stops until they close their eyes to rest at the end of the day.

It would be easy as a parent to be frustrated, angry, or demoralized. But the reality is we struggle just as much as our children with being unable to dial it down and turn it off. If we were honest with ourselves, we would admit that many times the noise gets so loud in our lives we can't even focus on our children or our own health.

If this sounds like your family, then it's time to create some margins in your life for technology-free moments. Quietness is good for your heart, your spirit, and your attitude. Allowing a mere twenty minutes in your day to go without screens will allow yourself to dwell on the things that are most important to you.

In the gospels there are several occasions we are told that Jesus *"went by himself to a mountainside to pray."* He knew the importance of quietness amidst the commotion of life.

Controlling Loose Lips

"Don't use foul or abusive language. Let everything you say be good and helpful, so that your words will be an encouragement to those who hear them."

Ephesians 4.29

Technology has made the spread of information lightning-fast.

Whether it is a politician caught in a scandal, a country being overthrown, or your child's school letting out early for snow—it only takes ten seconds for you to find out. Unfortunately, the same is true of gossip on social media.

Technology has created a carelessness with information for both children and parents. As a parent, it is imperative that you not use the web as a place to broadcast your frustrations or disappointments with other parents or authority figures. The same goes for sharing personal information about others. Another person's sin (including your child's) is his or her story to share and not yours.

A good exercise is to have your family agree that you will not use the web to demean, tease, or gossip about another person. It is too easy for feelings to get hurt and trust to be lost. You have an opportunity to help your child learn a different way to live out relationships online by speaking truth in love.

Finding Identity in the Proper Place

> *"Long ago, even before he made the world, God loved us and chose us in Christ to be holy and without fault in his eyes. His unchanging plan has always been to adopt us into his own family by bringing us to himself through Jesus Christ. And this gave him great pleasure."*
>
> Ephesians 1.4-5

One of the greatest struggles for teenagers is being able to enjoy who they are as people. They spend most of their time trying to fit in, earn the approval of adults they respect, and feel comfortable with themselves. In many ways social media has made this worse.

In many ways, teens have substituted real-life relationships for the instant gratification of someone else "liking" or "retweeting" something they've said online. One girl I spoke with said, "If I don't have at least one hundred 'likes' for my new pics on Instagram, I start thinking something is wrong."

Make sure that the affection and affirmation you are giving your child screams louder and more sincerely than anything she gets online. Talk with your children about who they are apart from their online lives. Help them to see their worth in Christ.

Avoiding Sexual Immorality

> "Let there be no sexual immorality, impurity, or greed among you. Such sins have no place among God's people."
> Ephesians 5.3

We have already covered in great detail the struggles that teenagers have with sex and technology. The elephant in the room that no one wants to talk about is that most adults struggle with sexuality and technology as well. It is just as easy for us as parents and grandparents to get pulled into chat rooms, websites, and unhealthy online flirting.

As the leader of your family, you need not only to talk with your children about these issues, but also to actively pray for your children's protection online. Pray that your daughter will find her beauty in who God declares her to be and not in the plastic photoshopped images she sees online. Pray that your son will choose to honor himself and others by turning from the artificial beauty of pornography.

Talk about purity with your children. It is about much more than pornography or sexualized women in video games. It is about a condition of the heart and the people they desire to be in public and private. Help them see that their purity can be expressed by what they post, gaze at, and seek after with technology.

Honoring Yourself and Others

"Don't just pretend that you love others. Really love them. Hate what is wrong. Stand on the side of the good. Love each other with genuine affection, and take delight in honoring each other."
Romans 12.9-10

Honor means to treat someone or something as if it has great value or worth. You show value to your children in the way that you touch them, look at them, speak to them, and spend time with them. When you allow technology to come between you and your relationship with your family members, plain and simple, it is dishonoring.

I was talking to a high school girl recently who said, "My parents are on screen just as much as I am. We don't talk as much as we used to because we are always staring at something else." When this happens in your own family, you raise the value of technology and lower the value of each other.

It is important that you teach your children how to use technology without ignoring one another. When your teenager's time with his video games or your time in front of your new Ultra High Definition TV takes the place of eye contact with one another, you know things have gone too far. Practice leaving devices in your pockets and out of sight when talking to one another or on a family outing.

I struggle with this myself. It is easy to lie to myself and say, "But this call is important," or "I really need to return this email." In reality, the attention from others feeds the broken parts of me. Instead, I'm learning that when I show my family that I *really love them,"* then they in turn *"take delight in honoring each other."*

In the end, your iPods will break, your children will want new video games, and there will be more emails to answer. Your love for one another is all that will truly remain. And that is good to know.

Notes

Chapter One - Controlling the Cell Phone Monster

1. The Importance of Family Dinners, 2012 Report, The National Center on Addiction and Substance Abuse at Columbia University, 2012.

2. Sex and Tech Report, The National Campaign to Prevent Teen and Unplanned Pregnancy, 2009.

3. Uhls, Y. T., & Greenfield, P. M. (2011, December 19). The Value of Fame: Preadolescent Perceptions of Popular Media and Their Relationship to Future Aspirations. *Developmental Psychology*.

Chapter Two - Got a Texting Addict at Your Home

1. Small, G., MD & Vorgan, G. (2008). *iBrain: Surviving the Technological Alteration of the Modern Mind*. New York, NY: William Morrow.

2. Weisskirch, R., PhD. "No Crossed Wires: Cell Phone Communication in Parent-Adolescent Relationships." *Cyberpsychology, Behavior, and Social Networking*. July/August 2011, 453-459.

Chapter Four - Video Game Violence and Moral Behavior

1. Lenhart, A. (2008). *Teens, Video Games, and Civics*. Pew Internet Project.

2. Anderson, C. A., Shibuya, A., Ihori, N., Swing, E. L., Bushman, B. J., Sakamoto, A., Rothstein, H. R., Saleem, M., & Barlett, C. P. (2010). Violent video game effects on aggression, empathy, and prosocial behavior in Eastern and Western countries: A meta-analytic review. *Psychological Bulletin*, 136(2), 151-173.

Chapter Nine - Helping Your Teen Protect Their Online Reputation

1. "Employers are Scoping Out Job Seekers on Social Media," www.CareerBuilder.com, 2012.

Chapter Eleven - The Dangerous Roulette of Video Chatting

1. Buhler, T., Neustaedter, C., & Hillman, S. (2013). "How and Why Teenagers Use Video Chat." School of Interactive Arts and Technology, Simon Fraser University.

Chapter Twelve - Cyberbullying: It's All the Rage

1. Do Something, "11 Facts About Bullying," www.dosomething.org

Chapter Thirteen - The Allure of Internet Pornography

1. Sabina, C., Ph.D., Wolak, J., J.D., & Finkelhor, D., Ph.D. (2008). "The Nature and Dynamics of Internet Pornography Exposure for Youth." *CyberPsychology & Behavior. 11* (6).

2. Sex and Tech Report, The National Campaign to Prevent Teen and Unplanned Pregnancy, 2009.

WEB-BASED RESOURCES

These are a few of the organizations that provide excellent articles and resources for you in your quest to become a tech savvy parent.

uknowkids.com - Looking for a way to keep tabs on your child's technology footprint? These guys have got the tools and great free ebooks to help.

CommonSenseMedia.org - This is a one-stop place for reviews from parents and teenagers on various kinds of media such as video games, movies, and TV.

PewInternet.org - The Pew Research Internet Project is the best place on the web of research and survey on how technology affects our lives.

ESRB.org - The Entertainment Software Rating Board website can quickly show you the rating and its explaination for virtually any video game.

StaySafeOnline.org - Protecting your child's online identity and reputation is paramount to these guys.

FOSI.org - The Family Online Safety Institute has created a "Platform for Good" that teaches parents to teach their kids to use technology for the benefit of all.

CovenantEyes.org - Covenant Eyes has created a program for one-on-one, ongoing web accountability.

XXXChurch.org - These guys have some of the best writing on sexual purity in regard to technology. Their blog will both encourage and challenge you.

StompOutBullying.org - Show this to your teen and talk about the issues together.

360Family.org - Brian Housman runs this family equipping organization.

Family Cell Phone Contract

The purpose of this contract is to make sure my parents and I are on the same page when it comes to how I will use my cell phone. This will help me earn their trust and confidence in my choices.

Teenager should initial each of the following sentences. Both parent and teen sign the contract.

_____ I agree that having a cell phone is a privilege and not a right guaranteed by the U.S. Constitution.

_____ I agree to no phone calls or texting after ___PM weekdays; ___PM week-ends, unless calls/texts are to my parent or person approved by my parent.

_____ I agree that I will keep my monthly text messaging limit within what is allowed by our family texting plan. Anything over that is my responsibility.

_____ I agree that I will not use my cell phone during dinner time or family time.

_____ I agree that I will initially be restricted from web browsing until the privilege is earned.

_____ I agree that any content I download, such as ringtones, music, apps, etc. must be approved by my parent and paid for by me at time of download.

_____ I agree that since my parents are paying for my phone, they have the right to look at my texts, apps, history, etc. If these items have been erased, then we have a problem.

_____ I agree that when I am out with my friends I will ALWAYS have my phone on so I can be reached by my parents. No excuses.

_____ I agree that if I'm asked to turn off/hand over my phone and don't do so in a reasonable amount of time, the phone could be torched, destroyed, donated, etc.

_____ I most certainly agree that if I show responsibility with my phone over a period of time, my parents may increase my freedoms.

_____ This contract will be reevaluated every six months as I get older to possibly receive more privileges.

Teen Signature _____ Date: _____

Parent Signature _____ Date: _____

ABOUT THE AUTHOR

Brian is a prolific writer for parenting magazines, most notably *Parenting Teenagers* and *Parent Life*. He publishes two blogs, "Conversations on Napkin" and "Tech Savvy Parenting." He is also the author of *Engaging Your Teen's World* and *Raising Responsible Teens in a Digital World*.

Brian and his wife, Mona, have been married for twenty-one years and have two teenagers of their own: a son, Bailey, and daughter, Ashlan. Besides loving and shaping their own teens, together they enjoy coaching other parents. Brian has served families for more than twenty-two years in a variety of positions including youth pastor, school administrator, teaching pastor, and camp director. Brian serves as the executive director for 360 Family, a nonprofit dedicated to encouraging and equipping parents to understand their teenagers, based in Memphis, TN.

Brian has had the privilege of speaking at more than 100 conferences and countless churches, schools, camps, and military bases. He has led student and parent programs from coast to coast as well as several international locations.

Interested in having Brian speak at your PTA/PTF, church group, parent conference, or family camp? Visit www.360family.org for more information.

D6 | CONFERENCE

a family ministry conference
connecting **CHURCH** and **HOME**
through generational discipleship